The Northern Navajo Frontier,
1860–1900

The Northern Navajo Frontier 1860–1900

Expansion through Adversity

Robert S. McPherson

Utah State University Press
Logan, Utah

Utah State University Press
Logan, Utah 84322

Manufactured in the United States of America

Printed on acid-free paper

08 07 06 05 04 03 02 01 1 2 3 4 5 6 7 8

Library of Congress Cataloging-in-Publication Data

McPherson, Robert S., 1947–
The northern Navajo frontier, 1860–1900 : expansion through adversity / Robert S. McPherson.
p. cm.
Originally published: Albuquerque : University of New Mexico Press, c1988.
Includes bibliographical references and index.
ISBN 0-87421-424-6 (alk. paper)
1. Navajo Indians. 2. Navajo Indians—Land tenure. 3. Frontier and pioneer life—Southwest, New. I. Title.
E99.N3 M34 2001
979.1004'972—dc21

2001046525

TABLE OF CONTENTS

PREFACE

The need for a history of the northern Navajo frontier has existed for a long time. Although writings about the Navajo are extensive, little detailed information has been published about the northern part of the reservation largely because it is considered peripheral to many of the tribe's major events. Early recorded histories of this area often portray the Navajo as either a helpless nuisance to the white settlements along the San Juan River or as aggressors who preyed upon lonely victims. Few authors have delved deeply enough to realize that the Navajo pursued a general course of action which allowed them not only to survive but at times to prosper during the Euro-American advance of the late nineteenth century frontier of the Four Corners area.

My interest in their story began in 1976, when I started working for the Utah Navajo Development Council, and later, as a teacher for the College of Eastern Utah—San Juan Campus. As snatches of Navajo stories from the old days started to surface, it became apparent that the people I worked with had both an intense interest and a strong cultural pride in the deeds of their forefathers. Unfortunately, the mists of time covered much of their history. The paucity of accurate, published information spurred a search that led to government records, oral histories, settlers' accounts, and public records. Because of the early time period under investigation (1860–1900), I depended heavily on written sources, but when feasible, I also interviewed and discussed with Navajo people living in the Four Corners area, the impressions received from information found in the documents. The result is, I hope, a book balanced in its presentation and judicious in its interpretation.

Special thanks is given to my mentors, Ted J. Warner and Thomas G.

Alexander, both of whom directed and encouraged the writing of the manuscript. Their insight and candid evaluation provided the pertinent questions and guidance necessary to bring it to fruition. Appreciation is also expressed to Kay Shumway, my supervisor, for making the time available for me to undertake this project. And finally, my love and admiration go to Betsy and the children, who learned to cope with my long hours away from home and the vacations never taken in order to complete this book. Much of the real credit goes to them.

Map 1. Navajo Reservation Boundaries.

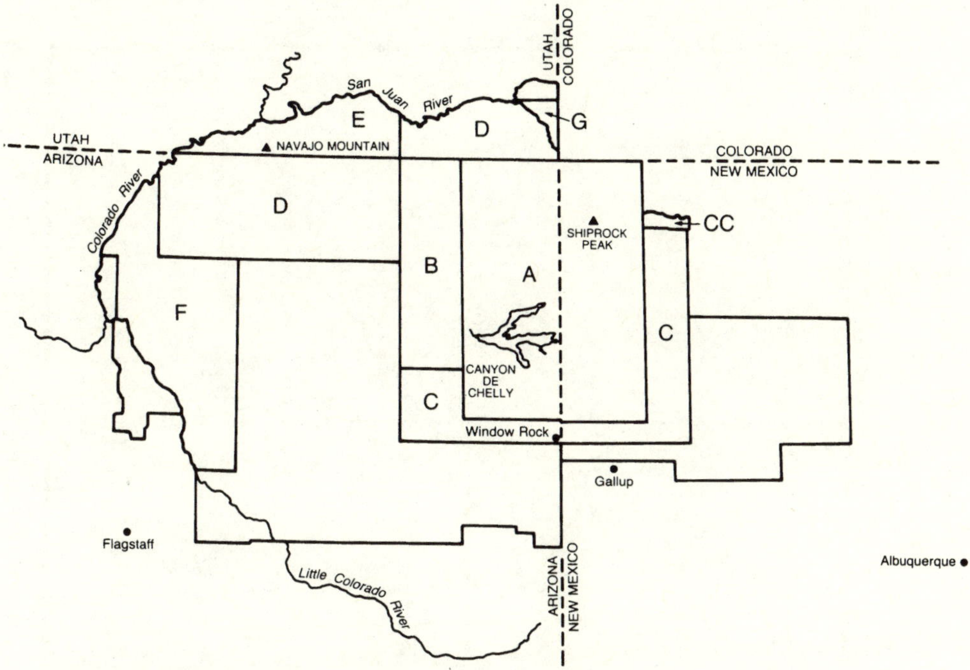

Source: Adapted from Peter Iverson, *The Navajo Nation* (University of New Mexico Press, 1981).

A Original treaty reservation. June 1, 1868.

B Executive-order addition. October 29, 1878.

C Executive-order addition. January 6, 1880.

CC Originally a part of "C"; withdrawn from the reservation by executive order, May 17, 1884; restored by executive order, April 24, 1886.

D Executive-order addition. May 17, 1884.

E The Paiute Strip. Originally a part of "D"; in 1892 restored to the public domain; in 1908 withdrawn for the use of various Indians.

F Executive-order addition. January 8, 1900.

G Executive-order addition. March 10, 1905.

Map 2. The Northern Navajo Frontier, 1860–1900.

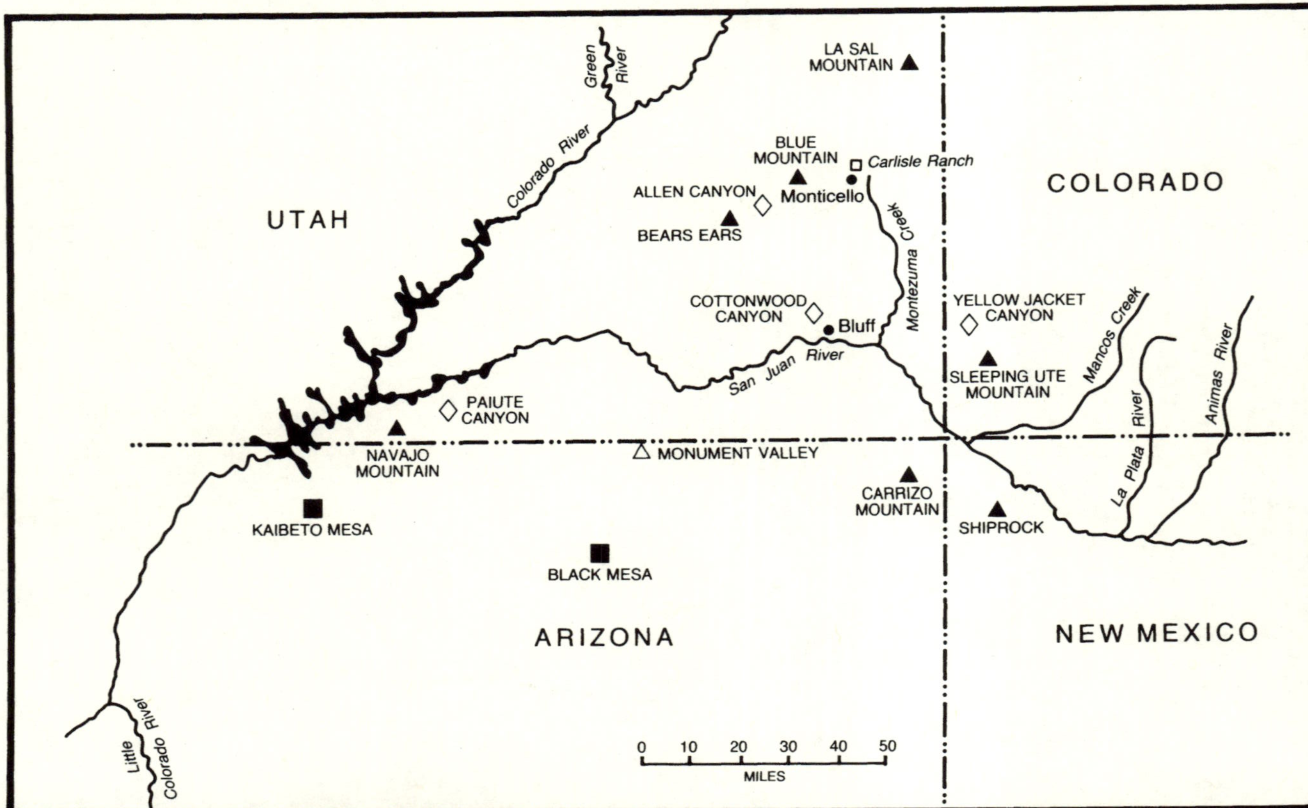

1 / Setting the Stage

The Navajo tribe is one of the most frequently researched groups of Indians in North America. Anthropologists, archaeologists, sociologists, and historians have taken turns explaining their views of Navajo history and culture. A recurrent theme throughout is that the U.S. government defeated the Navajos so soundly during the early 1860s that after their return from incarceration at Bosque Redondo, they were a badly shattered and submissive people.[1]

The next thirty years saw a marked demographic boom during which the Navajo population doubled. Historians disagree as to the extent of this growth, one author claiming a jump from 15,000 to 30,000 people by the beginning of the twentieth century, another placing the figures at 9,000 in 1868 and 21,000 by 1900.[2] Regardless of disagreement over the specific numbers, the position taken by many historians is that because of this growth and the rapidly expanding herds of sheep, cattle, and horses, the government beneficently gave more territory to its suffering wards.

While this interpretation is partly accurate, it centers on the role of the government, the legislation that was passed, and the frustrations of the Indian agents who rotated frequently through the Navajo Agency in Fort Defiance, New Mexico. One ethnohistorian, Klara B. Kelly, went so far as to interpret the Navajos' helplessness as part of a major attempt by the United States at "conquest, colonization and national oppression of the Navajo nation, spearheaded by U.S. mercantile and industrial capitalism."[3] Thus, she argues that the Navajos were enslaved by economic bondage, having little opportunity for self-determination.

Such views either ignore or severly limit one of the most important actors in this process of land acquisition—the Navajos themselves. Instead of being a downtrodden group of prisoners, defeated militarily in the 1860s and dependent on the U.S. government for protection and guidance in the 1870s and 80s, they were vigorously involved in defending and expanding the borders of their homelands. This was accomplished not through war and as a concerted effort, but by an aggressive defensive policy built on individual action that varied with changing circumstances. Thus, this book focuses on the events and activities in one part of the Navajo borderlands—the northern frontier—where between 1860 and 1900 the Navajos were able to secure a large portion of land that is still a part of the reservation. This expansion was achieved during a period when most Native Americans were losing their lands.

The term *frontier* is used here to describe the unsettled area of the Four Corners region during the mid-to-late nineteenth century. *Webster's Third New International Dictionary* defines this word as a part of a country that fronts or faces another country. In this instance, the Navajos confronted several "nations" along their borders: (1) the Ute/Paiute factions of southern Utah, southern Colorado, and northern New Mexico; (2) the Mormons with their attempts to carve a Kingdom of God out of the wilderness; and (3) an assortment of gentile, or non-Mormon, groups, including settlers, miners, and cowboys.

The area was truly a "shifting or advancing zone or region" as pioneer settlements, cattle companies, and mining operations moved into the country in tides that ebbed and flowed according to economic trends and government legislation. These Euro-Americans or "Anglos" came into the area because of the qualities of a frontier—"a new and relatively unexploited field that offered scope for large exploitative or developmental activity"—but many were discouraged by confronting the Navajos, who also desired to use the area, but for different reasons. Thus, the Four Corners region was in every sense a "frontier" to both the Indians and the Anglos.

The Navajos' success in obtaining this land is attested by eight boundary changes in their reservation that took place between 1868 and 1905, all of which occurred on this northern frontier (see Map 1). Here, *northern* is roughly defined by drawing an imaginary line from Farmington, New Mexico, through Shiprock to Kayenta, Arizona, and then dipping southwest to the Moenkopi/Tuba City region. The major area of concern is the Four Corners region, where a burst of activity erupted in the last half of the 1800s. The central focus is on southern Utah, the northernmost point of Navajo expansion and an area diverse in both geography and people.

The material is organized in the following manner. Chapter two looks at Ute and Paiute interaction with the Navajos between 1860 and 1880. This is a period about which historians have written a great deal concerning the Bosque Redondo experience, but have generally ignored the experience of those Navajos who remained at large in peripheral areas. Chapter three discusses Mormon expansion along the Little Colorado and San Juan Rivers during which an aggressive missionary policy by the Latter-day Saints encouraged friendly relations with the Navajos. Although the Mormons achieved some success, they eventually exchanged their religious zeal and helpful approach for the more characteristic attitudes of Euro-American Society, thus encouraging the Navajos and their agents to remove the Mormons from part of the expanding reservation.

But the Mormons were not the only ones to get in trouble. When they entered the Bluff area in 1880, a colorful and cantankerous gentile settler named Henry L. Mitchell was there to greet them. For the next five years, he was involved in continuous strife with his Navajo, Ute, and Mormon neighbors. His troubles form an interesting chronicle of conflict along the San Juan. Of all the gentile settlers in this region, Mitchell was the most vociferous, providing one of the fullest records of problems in this area. These problems are discussed in chapter four.

Chapter five discusses the role of the cattle companies in Utah and the pressure they put on natural resources used by the Indians. Although the cowboys were among the most hated of interlopers to both Utes and Navajos, they nevertheless were not the only ones to overstock the range and slaughter the deer. The Indians, in particular, were heavily involved in the sale of hides to traders, the topic of chapter six. Some trading posts manipulated the Navajos, but the Navajos also took advantage of the stores, flocking to the reservation boundaries to barter their wool, hides, blankets, and silver for commodities. No single institution did more to provide the Navajos with the goods they desired than the trading post, but it also created some difficult problems for the Indian agents. Uncontrolled trade led to conflict, creating an increased demand for clearly defined boundaries and tighter reins on both Navajos and Euro-Americans. The consolidation of the northern Navajo frontier is the subject of chapter seven. The establishment of the subagency at Shiprock in 1903 achieved this goal and made obsolete many of the old ways of solving problems. Navajo clashes with Utes, Mormons, gentile settlers, cowboys, and miners were now relegated to structured civilian organizations like courts and governmental proceedings instead of the military, as had been the case in the 1870s and 80s. This is not to suggest that the courts and the government were not involved earlier, or that the military was no longer involved, but only that a more organized, clearly defined, and peaceful means was established. When this happened, the frontier was closed. Chapter eight summarizes the findings of this study and suggests an interpretation of events based on a Navajo aggressive—defensive policy.

2 / Navajos, Utes and the Paiute Connection, 1860–80

"My grandson, do something for yourself," the old woman warned as she left the captive Navajo tied up in the Ute tepee. Twelve days had passed since his capture near the San Juan River and his prospects of survival were diminishing, as malnutrition and mistreatment took their toll. His captors were now sitting in council to decide his fate. But the Utes had not bargained for the intervention of the supernatural in the form of Quastceẹlci, a *Yeibichai* (Navajo for "god"), who put them to sleep as they talked and then helped the Navajo prisoner escape. Through a rough canyon, into a mountain, down a rat's hole, atop a mountain, and along a lightning path, the Navajo moved from the lands of the Ute to the safety of his people. Following this, he instructed the *Dine* (a Navajo term meaning "the People") in a ceremony that reiterated the knowledge gained during his flight and reenacted the events of his travels.[1]

This brief summary of the Mountain Chant recorded by Washington Matthews in 1887 is instructive for several reasons. First, it is one of the earliest versions of Navajo mythology, or sacred beliefs, to have been directly translated with an eye for accuracy. Second, the Mountain Chant holds in common with other Navajo myths and legends the thematic element of the Utes as antagonist.[2] Third, the narrative portrays the fine integration of the physical with the supernatural in its sanctifying of geography through mythology in the northern part of the Navajos' land and the western part of the Utes' domain. And finally, it shows the ambivalence in Navajo-Ute relations. When the Mountain Chant was first performed, the Navajos sent a courier to the north to invite, among other Indian groups, "some friendly bands of Ute."[3] This seeming inconsistency of friendly Utes and enemy Utes is a continuing theme in Navajo history, especially in the northern regions of Arizona and New Mexico and the southern parts of Utah and Colorado.

This chapter considers the relations between Navajos, Utes, and Paiutes in the northern part of what is today the Navajo Reservation and portrays their interaction during the period 1860–80, one of the most turbulent in the tribes' history.

The geographical location called the Four Corners area is noted for both its variety and roughness. Red rock canyons standing above desert sands quickly give way to towering alpine mountain peaks. These mountains—La Sal, Abajo, Sleeping Ute, Navajo Mountain, Chuska, and Carrizo—are collecting points for winter snows and summer rains, providing runoff to the parched basins and canyons below. Add to this the San Juan, Colorado, Little Colorado, Animas, and La Plata Rivers and two large plateaus—Black Mesa and Kaibeto— and one has a land of dramatic beauty but slow travel, inaccessibility, and protection for those who want to escape an enemy.

By the 1860s, escape was the goal of many Native American groups. Pressures from the east in Colorado, created by a series of mining strikes in the late 1850s and 1860s, encouraged some of the Utes to modify their lifestyle, relinquish their lands, and relocate further to the west in southwestern Colorado. The Paiutes, on the other hand, living in western Utah, eastern Nevada, and parts of northern Arizona, felt increasing pressure from Mormon settlements. By 1864, Mormons were located in at least four ranching and farming communities—Short Creek, Pipe Springs, Moccasin, and Kanab—assuming control over the best natural resources for their own use. They relocated the Paiutes to places outside these settlements, thus forming a protective ring and early warning system to aid the Mormons against Navajo and Ute depredations.[4]

To the south in New Mexico and Arizona, military operations, civilian forays, and Ute attacks exerted pressure against the Navajo to stop their raiding. Attempts to capture, kill, or bring about a peaceful settlement with the Navajos culminated during the early 1860s in the efforts of General James H. Carleton and Kit Carson. The trauma of the "long walk," the incarceration of the Navajos at Bosque Redondo (1864–68), and their subsequent release were all critical moments in tribal history. These events also served as a clarification of Euro-American–Navajo policy, which was implemented with varying degrees of success for the next sixty years.

While the Bosque Redondo period and the events leading to it have been adequately studied elsewhere, a large gap still remains in understanding what happened to those Navajos who did not go to Fort Sumner and their relationships with other tribal groups.[5] In order to piece together a badly fragmented story, one needs to realize that the area north of an imaginary line drawn through present-day Farmington, Shiprock, Kayenta, and Tuba City was used by three Native American groups—Utes, Navajos, and Paiutes (see Map 2).

The San Juan Band Paiutes hunted and gathered in southeastern Utah in a territory considered peripheral to most Paiute activity, though their presence was perhaps felt in this region as early as 1300 A.D.[6] In defining the boundaries of the San Juan Band, Isabel T. Kelly suggests as the limits of their domain "roughly, the area extended from Monument Valley to the Little Colorado and from the San Juan River to Black Mesa and Moencopi Plateau, without including either of the latter."[7] Robert C. Euler's *Southern Paiute Ethnohistory* mentions a number of contacts with Spanish, Mexican, and American military personnel and travelers in this same region, especially around the Navajo Mountain area.[8] By the 1860s Paiutes were being squeezed out of their territory in southwestern Utah and into the less hospitable territory of southeastern Utah and northern Arizona.

Much of the land into which they moved was claimed by the Weeminuche Utes, who lived along the San Juan River in southeastern Utah and who shared friendly relations with the Capote Utes. The Capote Utes ranged through northern New Mexico and southern Colorado. Though the Utes were Numic speakers like their Paiute cousins, the former thought themselves better than the latter and committed their energies to a profitable Paiute slave trade during the 1700s and 1800s.[9] The Utes also included the Navajos as targets for their slave raids, although there were attempts at alliance in 1855.[10] As Euro-American encroachment put pressure on the Utes to the east, agencies were organized in Conejos, Colorado, for the more eastern bands and at Abiquiu, New Mexico, for the Capote, Mouache, and Weeminuche in the early 1860s. The Weeminuche at this point were the least threatened of these groups because of their use of southeastern Utah, which was not under the direct influence of Euro-Americans.

Both the Paiutes and the Utes at this time lived in loosely organized bands in which membership was fluid. There was little formal leadership beyond the warrior who proved himself an able hunter, a skilled fighter, and a wise leader for his family and those who chose to follow him. Thus, like the Navajo, the Weeminuche Utes and the San Juan Paiutes operated on a small scale at a local level, with no centralized organization to direct activities. This is not to suggest that these groups were ineffective, but only that a unified policy between groups was usually nonexistent.

The Navajos also ranged throughout southeastern Utah, partly because of the good grazing areas on the mountainsides and along the streams for their herds of sheep and partly because of the agricultural opportunities offered by the rivers' flood plains. But during the late 1850s and early 1860s, as Ute and Euro-American contact with the Navajos increased, a period of trauma—the "Fearing Time"—descended upon the Dine. The hostilities generated during this era are well known among the older people even today. Ute raids conducted across the San Juan into the southern portion of Utah and northern part of Arizona and New Mexico pushed the Navajos into the more inaccessible parts of the territory. One reconnaissance made by Captain J. G. Walker into the northwestern part of Navajo land in 1859 found that although the area had been used as a refuge in the past, it was now abandoned because of "Pah Utah" (Paiute) activites. Walker, however, recognized the inherent defensive qualities of the region when he noted that "discovering their [Navajos'] hiding places would be as difficult as it was to discover Seminoles in the hummocks of Florida."[11] This factor of seclusion would become increasingly important.

It is interesting to note that the Army's commanding officer in New Mexico, playing on Ute-Navajo hostilities, shifted his policy from fostering peaceful coexistence to one of belligerency. For instance, in 1860 Colonel T. F. Fauntleroy requested the use of 300 Utes to serve against the Navajos "as they do not require pay as soldiers but only to be supplied a short time with provisions until they can get well into the Indian country . . . It will at once have the effect to get the cooperation of a most valuable force and at the same time employ these restless people, who otherwise must foray upon our own settlements."[12] Thus the Ute-Navajo war served a dual purpose for Americans in that it not only helped eliminate part of the Navajo menace but also occupied the Southern Utes.

Yet it was not only the Utes who attacked the Navajo. New Mexicans with Pueblo allies also brought the fight to Navajo country, seeking slaves and booty. Volunteer units penetrated into the heart of the region, capturing prisoners or just pushing the Navajos out of their homelands. The results of many of these raids were not recorded, but one group reported seizing a large corn crop, 100 captives, and 5,000 sheep and horses.[13] This was certainly a profitable way to fight a war, so these activities continued throughout the 1860s, even after the roundup of Navajos conducted by Kit Carson.

Naturally, the Dine retaliated against their adversaries, so that by 1861 they had "compelled the abandonment of the San Juan and Rio de las Animas gold mines . . . . Forty Americans and fifteen Mexicans were slaughtered upon the road and their property taken by the Navajos."[14] Navajo raids against the Utes also continued, but they were not enough to relieve the relentless pressure that pushed the Navajos into peripheral areas. Carson's drive through the northern part of the reservation merely continued a process that was already well under way. The Navajos respected and feared the Utes much more than the white soldiers working under Carson's command, since the Indian allies had a much better understanding of Navajo camp sites and herding and farming patterns.

With this background, it is easier to understand the evolution of Navajo and Ute relations and the role that the Paiutes played in mediating a bitter situation with those who did not go to Fort Sumner. Southeastern Utah and northern Arizona served as a gathering place for many Navajos looking for a sanctuary from the pressures of war. Navajo oral tradition is rich with stories of battles, slave raids, and flights into the wilderness. Sally Draper, in an interview in 1961, told how, in her great-grandmother's time, a band of Navajos, fleeing from a group of Utes and Mexicans, climbed atop a high bluff in the area of Red Mesa, Arizona. Surrounded by the enemy, parched with thirst and with no avenue of escape, they turned to supernatural help. The Navajos performed "Enemy Way" medicine, directing an evil power against their foe that killed the Ute leader and allowed the Navajos to escape.[15]

A more detailed account exists of a key individual named Hashkeneinii, who lived in the Monument Valley-Navajo Mountain area. With the approach of Carson and his Ute allies, Hashkeneinii gathered together a band of eight women, four men, and four children and fled north to the San Juan River. Traveling both night and day, driving a small herd of sheep before them, and avoiding the normal watering places by drinking from rock basins filled with rain water, they moved first to the San Juan River and then west to a crossing point that allowed them to enter the Navajo Mountain region. By this time Hashkeneinii had earned his name, generally translated as "Giving Out Anger," because of the relentless way he drove his family. Fear of the Utes caused him to push still deeper into the remote recesses on the southern side of Navajo Mountain where he formed a small village that remained in use for four years. Other Navajos, some of whom he found in the Kayenta area, joined him and helped gather stock scattered by the invading forces. The success of this hiding place is attested to by Hashkeneinii, who claimed that in the entire time he spent there before returning to Monument Valley in 1868, he met only one Ute man, who was friendly and more interested in trading than in warfare.[16]

One important point to consider in understanding Hashkeneinii's and other Navajos' experiences during this period of turmoil is the influence that wealth had upon their ability to survive. Called by some authors *ricos*—the Spanish term for "rich person"—men of wealth were often selected as leaders or *na' taani* because of their ability to ensure the physical prosperity of themselves and those who voluntarily allied with them.[17] Thus, Hashkeneinii influenced ten other Navajos to accompany him back to his camp and to work together for protection and mutual benefit. Hashkeneinii emerges as both the richest and the most influential man of this period, owning a large herd of sheep and a healthy store of silver.[18]

But Hashkeneinii was not an isolated case. Daghaa Sik' aad in the Kaibeto area, K' aayelii near the Bears Ears, and Spane Shank in the Navajo Mountain region were some of the better known of these headmen. A report in October 1864 further established that it was the wealthy Navajo who were able to avoid the trials at Fort Sumner. The Superintendent of Indian Affairs in New Mexico stated that "less than one-half the tribe have surrendered; that the prisoners embrace the poor, while the strength and wealth of the tribe remain in the western part of their country. . . . It is the opinion of those best informed as to their resources that it will take years to entirely subdue and remove them, as those still running at large are well mounted, well armed, have stock to live upon, and are the bravest and most warlike of the tribe.[19]

Perhaps the most famous of these ricos was Manuelito, who was born near the Bears Ears in Utah but by the time of Bosque Redondo lived in the area of the Little Colorado. General Carleton was aware of Manuelito's location, and though there were already too many Navajos at Fort Sumner for the Army to feed, clothe, and shelter, Carleton still attempted after some hesitation to get even more to surrender. On January 26, 1865, he sent a runner to confront Manuelito with an order to head for the fort so that he could arrive in time for the planting season. The ensuing report of this visit stated that "Manuelito answered that he would not leave his country; that he was doing no harm to anyone, and he intended to die there; that he had no fears and did not intend to run away. . . . The interpreter says there are from 400 to 600 horses and from 2,000 to 3,000 sheep owned by this band; that there are six so called "ricos;" that there are from twenty to thirty warriors, not more, and from 60 to 100 old and young, all told."[20] Thus, Manuelito's defiance was based principally on his economic well-being and only secondarily on his military strength.

At the end of this same report, an ominous note presaged the fate of Manuelito's band: "There have lately come from the Coconino Mountains, three rancherias, say thirty souls. One of these Indians was about the largest stock owner in the Navajo country but the Utes cleaned him out, leaving him only six horses. This party is on their way to this post, and will probably be here in about ten days."[21] One month later, in March 1865, Carleton sent Herrera Grande, a friend of Manuelito's, to survey the situation. He saw a decimated camp, its people scattered by Ute raids, its herd reduced to fifty horses and about the same number of sheep, and women who wept at the mention of the Utes. Manuelito complained bitterly as he pointed out, "Here is all I have in the world. See what a trifling amount. You see how poor we are. My children are eating roots."[22]

But he offered a brave front, persisting in his desire to remain free. Besides explaining that his livestock were too weak to make the trip to Fort Sumner, he also pointed out that his mother and his god lived in the west and that he would not leave either one. He then went on to say "that there was a tradition that his people should never cross the Rio Grande, the Rio San Juan or the Rio Colorado; that he also could not pass three mountains and particularly could he not leave the Chuska Mountains, his native hills; that his intention was to remain; that he was there to suffer all the consequences of war or famine."[23] In only a few months, however, Manuelito came in to surrender, after suffering near starvation, a devasted economic base and constant harassment by raiding Utes.

By August 20, 1866, Carlton reported that there were 6,915 Navajos at the Bosque with a new party of more than 100 Navajos having just arrived. "They were naked, sickly-looking and had the appearance of being starved.

They reported that their people, now in their old country, are in a starving and destitute condition; that they were constantly being harassed by the troops and Indians hostile to them; that they could not raise any crops and that all would come to the reservation if permitted to do so. I am of the opinion that nearly all those running at large will come to the reservation before winter sets in."[24]

But what about those who evaded capture, particularly those in the northern part of the Navajo domain? Logic suggests that in the Four Corners area and in southern Utah especially, because of its close proximity to Ute territory, strong pressure was put on the Navajos. In some instances, this was undoubtedly true. However, there were additional social, economic, and political forces encouraging at least a partial cessation of enmity between the Navajos and Utes. This situation was due to the Paiutes. To understand the reason, one needs to return to the events preceding the "Fearing Time." David Brugge, a noted historian, suggests the possibility that as early as 1823, during a campaign by Jose Antonio Vizcarra, the Paiutes helped the Navajos by concealing their location, allowing the Navajos to flee across the San Juan River with their herds.[25]

Yet it was not just in wartime that these relations became cemented. The Navajo considered the Paiute a poor tribe and not a military threat. The Paiutes herded sheep, did camp chores, and at times sold their children to Navajos to be used for labor.[26] By the late 1850s, the Paiutes' role among the Navajos increased, though still handled on an individual or family level, as both groups felt continuing pressure from white encroachment. Many Paiutes adopted the Navajo language, style of dress, and the practice of intermarriage.[27] They often established camps near Navajo settlements where trading and mutual support flourished. And though the Navajos looked down on the Paiutes, they considered them useful in performing tasks in exchange for which they received food. This symbiotic relationship occurred in not one but several locations—in Paiute Canyon, near Paiute Farms, along the San Juan River, by the Bears Ears, on Blue Mountain, and near Monument Valley.[28]

This compatibility and cooperation was noticed by others in the area. During the late 1850s, as the Mormons in southwestern Utah became increasingly concerned with the advance of Albert Sidney Johnston's army, the events connected with the Mountain Meadow Massacre, and the instability created by Ute raids, they desired to form an Indian alliance to shield them from possible harm. As early as January 1858 reports started to filter back through military channels that the Navajos and Utes in the northern part of the reservation were making peace, with the encouragement of the Mormons.[29] Fear of this new friendship caused claims of Navajo and Ute raiding and conflicts to arise.[30] These subsided as the Utes reported through Kit Carson that they had no desire to join the Mormons, but in fact wanted to wage an intense conflict against both them and the Navajos.[31]

The most interesting part of this incident was the continuing role played by the Paiutes, who acted as mediators between the Mormons, the Navajos, and other tribes. Captain J. G. Walker reported camping near the San Juan and Little Colorado rivers where a party of Paiutes, one of whom could speak the Navajo language fluently, gave the following statement:

> That the Mormons had deputed them and some others who had gone to the Canon de Chelly, to meet the Navajos and to make peace with them; that they (the Mormons) were anxious to see peace established between all the different tribes between the Colorado and the Rio Grande, and by that means resist the encroachment of the people and the government of the United States, the natural enemies of the whole Indian race. . . . The Mormons had sent them (the Pah Utahs) to invite the Navajos to meet them and all the different bands of the Utahs and the Mohaves at the Sierra Panoche [Navajo Mountain]. . . . This council is to be held about the middle of October next, at which time the Mormons are to distribute arms and ammunition to the various tribes represented in the council who join the alliance.[32]

Thus, Paiute fluency in Navajo, familiarity with the terrain, and friendly demeanor played a part in the decision to use them as middlemen between Utes, Navajos, and Mormons. It is also interesting that Navajo Mountain was selected as the meeting spot, since at this time it was not under the sovereignty of any one tribe.

As Ute pressures increased during the 1860s, the Navajos made greater use of the Paiutes. Beyond cooperation in daily life, they provided a lookout service to protect Navajo camps. For instance, K'aayelii lived in the Bears Ears area where he established a settlement of five or six hogans. To prevent surprise attacks, he posted Paiutes along the various approaches to his camp.[33] This same technique was employed in the Navajo Mountain area, with one informant saying that the Navajos there were "hiding behind" the Paiute.[34] The extent of this friendship may never be known precisely, because of a paucity of written records and conflicting oral testimony, but its existence cannot be questioned.

Paiute-Navajo relations were not always oriented toward peace and the avoidance of conflict. Occasionally the two groups united to raid profitable targets in their area, the most notable ones being the Mormon settlements of southwestern Utah. In 1866, a band of twenty-five Paiutes and Navajos came from the Navajo Mountain area and killed Dr. J. M. Whitmore and Alexander McIntyre near Pipe Springs. For the next three years, raiding activity intensified to the point that settlements on the eastern border were evacuated. Each fall a 200-mile stretch of land—from Beaver to St. Thomas, Utah—was attacked, with a total of six whites and a number of friendly Paiutes killed, and 500 horses, 500 cattle, and 2,000 sheep seized by the raiders.[35] Not all of the

Navajos were happy about these events, claiming that the raids were made by young men who used false reasons like hunting or trading expeditions to disguise their real intent.[36] The important point, however, is that Navajos and Paiutes worked together in this border warfare that continued into the 1870s.

During this same period, a problem existed in distinguishing between Utes and Paiutes in southeastern Utah. Slight variations in language, larger variations in lifestyle, and overlapping subsistence areas, combined with the slave trade and intermarriage, created a blending of the two groups that exists to the present day. Paiutes from the ephemeral San Juan Band foraged for food well within the hunting and gathering areas claimed by the Weeminuche Band of Utes. Government reports, settlers' journals, and even the Ute Agencies at times differed in their reporting of these groups, calling them *Pah Utes, Pah Utahs, Payuches, Pi Utes, Pah Wymins, Wymin Utes, Guignimuche*, and *Womenuche.* Perhaps the best way to make sense out of this confusion is to realize that the predominant group in southeastern Utah was the Weeminuche Ute, to whom was attached through marriage part of the San Juan Band Paiute. These Paiutes were never accorded full status with other Ute bands, and even today the Weeminuche group located at Towaoc are looked down upon by other Utes as a mixture of Ute and Paiute, while the members of the White Mesa-Allen Canyon Ute groups, who are of Ute-Paiute ancestry, are viewed by those at Towaoc as an even more mixed breed. The importance of this lies in the fact that the Weeminuche of southeastern Utah have often been considered peripheral to the main activity of other Ute bands.

During this period, when Ute and Navajo warfare was so intense, the Weeminuches participated in raiding, yet at the same time developed ties of friendship with certain Navajo groups. For instance, as early as 1858, a captive Mexican, who was freed from Navajo control north of the Carrizo Mountains, claimed that one group of Navajos made peace with the Utes and "removed their whole band into the country north of the San Juan."[37]

But perhaps the most dramatic proof of Ute, Paiute, and Navajo cooperation came a few years later, during the height of Ute antagonism toward the Navajos. In September 1866, a group of Capote and Weeminuche Utes and a few Mexicans met for the purpose of organizing a ruse to trap a group of Navajos who had avoided going to Bosque Redondo and were presently living in northern Arizona. The plan was to send word that the Utes wanted to live in peace and in close proximity to them; after the Navajos arrived, the Utes would kill the men, enslave the women and children, and capture the livestock. Upon hearing this plan, however, Cabeza Blanca, a Weeminuche leader, disagreed with the others, saying that he had friends among those Navajos whom he did not want to have killed. A fight ensued, during which the Capotes killed Cabeza Blanca and then fled to Tierra Amarilla for protection. Although the sons of Cabeza Blanca never caught their father's killers, they did kill three herders and wounded a woman—all Mexicans—and seized some livestock along the Chama River.

The government report of this incident said that "the Indians then left, joining as is supposed the Wymin and Pah Utes who had made friends with the Navajos in the meantime. The whole party of Wymin, Pah Utes, and Navajos then left that region and went to the neighborhood of Rio Dolores, Sierra Salir [La Sal Mountains], and Sierra Orejos [Bears Ears]."[38] Major Albert Pfeiffer, the author of the letter, wrote that he wanted the Capotes to make peace with the Weeminuche so that they could "deliver up to me the Navajos who were with the Wymin Utes that they might be sent to the Bosque; that in case the Navajos (their enemies) refused to go, I would lead them in a campaign against that tribe; that the government desired the Wymin, Pah and Capote Utes to bury the hatchet and be friends and that only one of their tribe had been killed and that this could be easily settled." Pfeiffer also mentioned that if this bid for peace was not achieved, a war might result that would destroy Tierra Amarilla and surrounding settlements. He estimated that the hostile force that could be brought together to wage this conflict could include 1,200 Weeminuches, 1,500 Paiutes, and about 800 Navajos.

While these fears were never realized, and no massive outbreak occurred, this incident is instructive for a number of reasons. First, it shows that ties between the Navajos, Paiutes, and Utes were strong—so strong that Weeminuches turned against Capotes to the point of bloodshed. Second, the three groups were located in southeastern Utah—a place of general use for all three of these tribes. Third, this was one of the first reports to identify a triumvirate that for the next thirty years comprised those considered renegades and troublemakers not only by the whites moving into southeastern Utah but also by many leaders from their own tribes.

The Capotes continued to wage a brushfire war against their brothers the Weeminuches with sporadic instances of bloodshed in 1866 and 1868.[39] Weeminuche ties to the Navajos were again stressed during a conference held at Pagosa Springs near the San Juan, when the Utes pointed out that Capote raids had caused Navajo retaliation but that the Weeminuches would fight only to defend themselves if necessary.[40]

And yet to characterize Weeminuche and Navajo relations during the 1860s as totally pacific is incorrect. Certain bands attacked the Navajos while others maintained friendships. For instance, one leader named Persechopa, desired peace between his people and the Navajos. When horse stealing by the latter offered justification for a return raid, Persechopa instead went to the Navajo Agency asking that the horses be given back and the peace maintained. Upon returning home, he died of dropsy which the Utes claimed was a result of Navajo poisoning, and thus grounds for war.[41] Three months later some Navajos stole four horses from a group of Capotes who then retrieved them at the expense of one Ute and possibly as many as six Navajos killed.[42] Sebo, a

Weeminuche leader, accompanied the Capotes on this trip and even went in and talked with the Navajos before the fighting started.

On the other hand, many Navajos still remember a gray-haired Ute, perhaps Cabeza Blanca, who roamed the Four Corners area and was extremely effective in capturing Navajo women, children, and livestock.[43] He was noted for being well-armed, persistent, and knowledgeable in ferreting out his enemies from their hiding places; he sold women captives to Mexicans.

What was the justification for this seeming inconsistency of at one point raiding Navajos and at another fighting to protect the same people? While documentation is sparse, the activities of the 1860s indicate that this was a period of increased interaction between Utes, Paiutes, and Navajos because of pressure from white encroachment. Further, the ties of the Paiutes to the Utes in language and through intermarriage brought these two groups closer together. In a spatial sense, this joined the Paiutes from the west with the Utes from the east. Likewise, the Navajos from the southern part of the Four Corners area were tied with the Paiutes to their north and west. Marriage of Paiutes to Navajos and of Paiutes to Utes created kinship ties that, though weak, found fruition first in trading negotiations and later, as the three groups became more friendly, in other forms of support. Although the Paiutes were gradually being assimilated into both Ute and Navajo culture, the Utes and Navajos remained distinctly separate and at times antagonistic toward each other. Thus, it is not suggested that there was a strong amalgamation as much as there was an easing of tension in this part of the reservation.

Trading has often been a means of softening animosity between warring Native American groups. Oral histories indicate that several areas along the San Juan River were used as trading spots between Utes and Navajos.[44] The vicinity of present-day Montezuma Creek, White Rocks south of Bluff, and a spot by the Bears Ears, were all trading places frequented by Utes, Paiutes, and Navajos to exchange goods. Even during times of war, trading expeditions were given safe-conduct to their places of business.[45] Items traded by the Utes included buckskins, buckskin clothing, elk hides and elk storage sacks, buffalo robes, saddlebags, horses, bandoleers, beaded bags, beaver skins, buffalo tails for rattles, pitch for ceremonial whistles, and baskets. The Navajos traded woven blankets, silver, and agricultural products.[46] The Navajo Mountain area provided a red earth paint sold by the Paiutes to the Utes.[47] Mention is also made of Paiutes from this area visiting Paiutes near the Bears Ears in order to obtain buckskins.[48]

The trading expeditions were often as much of a religious nature as they were an opportunity for economic exchange. Songs from the "Blessing Way" ceremony were sung by the Navajos to ensure successful bargaining and a safe return, especially when venturing beyond the San Juan River, a part of the northern Navajo boundary. A ceremonial name—Dwellers-in-the-Cedar-Bark—was used to describe the Utes in order to summon supernatural aid, while the main event of trading was accompanied by the taboo that Navajo men could not sleep with Ute women. An account of an 1870 trading expedition to the northern Utes contained the remark that it was better trading with the people in the north than it was with the people around Sleeping Ute Mountain, because those Utes had "crows" and "coyotes" amongst them.[49] Yet trading persisted, and William H. Jackson reported a Weeminuche trading expedition loaded with furs, traveling to the Navajos by way of Yellow Jacket Canyon in southwestern Colorado.[50] Often traders from the two tribes had a sponsor or "friend," or trading partnership that was maintained between two families for several generations. Thus it seems likely that some Utes, Paiutes, and Navajos established strong bonds by trading along the San Juan.

Kinship was another source for strengthening relationships. Several Navajo families in the Navajo Mountain-Monument Valley area claim Paiute ancestry originating during this period.[51] Ute and Paiute intermarriage also occurred during the same time, the results of which are seen at least in part in the White Mesa-Allen Canyon Ute community today. In the early 1900s, the Ute censuses from Towaoc show a strong mixture of Ute and Paiute families that had been established long before the censuses were taken.[56] Kinship ties, therefore, from Ute-Paiute and Navajo-Paiute marriages in at least some instances had a mellowing effect on Ute-Navajo antagonism.

Events in the 1870s reveal just how close these kinship bonds were. The label of "renegade" was attached to the amalgamation of San Juan Paiutes with parts of the Weeminuche Utes. A Navajo agent, James H. Miller, left Fort Defiance looking for irrigable lands along the San Juan River. He was attacked and killed in camp on June 11, 1872, by a group initially identified as Utes.[53] The criminals were next reported to be among the Paiutes in Utah, while Ouray, a Tabeguache Ute, promised to deliver the guilty parties to the government.[54] A year later the Utes reported killing the murderers.[55] If true this incident illustrates that the Utes regarded this Paiute-Ute faction as a renegade group and gave them no protected status.

Soon after this, two incidents marred the uneasy peace on the northern Navajo frontier. First, a force of Navajos and Paiutes attacked a group of miners traveling on a road along the Utah-Arizona border near Needle Rock. The miners suggested that this same group of Indians killed three Mormons near Mountain Meadows, Utah.[56] Again, in March 1874 three Navajos who had been drying beef obtained from Utes near Circle Valley, Utah, were killed, while a fourth Navajo escaped to tell the story. Relations grew bitter as the Navajos demanded a large payment from the Mormons, though in reality the murderers were non-Mormons.[57] Jacob Hamblin, a Mormon frontiersman famous for his ability to work with Indians, visited the Navajo camp at Navajo Mountain and almost lost his life there.[58] One interesting aspect of this affair is that Hamblin believed he had been betrayed by a Paiute interpreter who promised the Navajos horses and cattle from the Mormons.[59]

In 1875, the Ute-Paiute faction attacked the Ferdinand V. Hayden Survey Party, and Ouray sounded the familiar cry of renegades, saying the deed was committed by a "little patriarchal band of outlaw . . . Paiutes." Others later admitted that it was actually a group of Weeminuches living near the La Sal Mountains.[60] About this same time, Navajos, Weeminuches, and Paiutes were reported to be camping together on the La Plata River.[61]

Two years later, because of reservation boundary problems with settlers, the Utes in the southwestern part of their reservation prepared for war and went to the Navajo Reservation to recruit help. The Navajo agent stated that "there are a few Navajos, who I fear will listen to the councils of the Utes," so he sent word for all of his charges to return to the reservation.[62]

This call to return upset a number of Navajos who had established themselves as sharecroppers on Ute lands along the La Plata River. Their arrangement of growing corn annually and sharing it with the Utes who "rented" the land worked well, so there was little motivation to return to the reservation. The agent, therefore, gave permission for those Navajos married to Utes to remain with that tribe.[63] Navajo and Ute ties of friendship were strengthened so that when it was time to hand out annuities and rations at the Los Pinos Agency in Colorado, 44 Navajos arrived along with 358 Utes.[64]

Perhaps the most significant and instructive incident to illustrate Navajo, Ute, and Paiute relations occurred in Monument Valley in 1880. In February of that year, reports of a double murder started to filter in to Navajo Agent Galen Eastman. A Navajo named "Boy with Many Horses" mentioned that while visiting a Paiute camp sixty miles above Lee's Ferry, he had seen four pack mules that were said to belong to two murdered white men. This type of occurrence was fairly common in the area, and often the Navajos were blamed for action taken by Paiutes. The agent ordered an investigation.[65] Within a week, Eastman received a letter from Henry L. Mitchell, the father of one of these missing men, saying that his son should have returned home to Riverside [Aneth area] a month ago and that the Navajos and Utes were acting "sausy" (*sic*)—the latter claiming that in the spring they would try to drive the white men out of their hunting grounds and grazing areas.[66] Mitchell responded to this threat by saying that within six weeks there would be 200 men ready to do battle with the troublemakers. Two weeks later a letter from Mitchell arrived in Washington, sent to Secretary of the Interior Carl Schurtz, complaining that Eastman was six months late in ordering the Navajos back to their reservation; that during this time horses and cattle had been stolen or killed; that Mitchell had just returned from retrieving the bones of his son and Charles Merrick who had been ambushed in Monument Valley; that the Navajos claimed the Utes had done it and the Utes claimed the Navajos had done it but that the blame for the crime rested on the Navajo. Mitchell then recommended that a company of soldiers be sent, to capture not only the recalcitrant Navajos but also some Utes, who had recently been involved in the White River Massacre.[67] He wrote another letter to Eastman saying that Navajos and Utes had killed not only the two already reported, but five more men whose bodies had not yet been found. He then indignantly told Eastman, "If you can't take care of those Indians, let us know quick, for if there is not something done, you won't have any Navajos, for there will be in less than 90 days, some 1,000 men here; we can kill just as well as they can and we do not intend to be run over any longer. The Navajos are terrors, cutthroats, thieves and murderers."[68]

A report of this incident was published in the *Denver Tribune* dated March 17, 1880. Entitled "Indian Imps: The Work of Butchery and Bloodshed Goes on," the article reported the gory details of the murders; stated that Utes, Navajos, and Paiutes were to blame; and then suggested that Mormons in the area were providing repeating rifles to the offenders. The reporter noted a close association among the Indians: "There has been an unusual friendship existing between the Southern Utes and Navajos. They have been passing backwards and forwards all winter, which in and of itself is a very suspicious circumstance. The Utes are more daring in their depredations than usual."[69] Although some of these claims were far-fetched—Mormons providing rifles and additional murders that had not occurred—it is interesting that Navajo-Ute relations were seen as being bonded during this period.

Agent Galen Eastman dispatched a delegation of reputable chiefs to look into the situation, but in the meantime, he received still another letter from Mitchell saying that his own investigation revealed that the murders had been committed by "Utes, some renegade Navajos and other contiguous Indians." Captain F. T. Bennett of the Ninth Cavalry was also conducting an investigation, sending a Mexican named Jesus with a Navajo to Moenkopi. Here, they were told by five Paiutes that four Utes, married to Paiute women, had killed the prospectors. "The Paiutes also said that the Utes said that their chiefs who went to Washington instructed all Ute Indians that if they (the Ute Chiefs) did not return in four months, that all Utes should kill all Americans they could. One of these five Paiutes named Bo-woos-Kush-ie, spoke good Navajo".[70] The report went on to say that "the Navajo Indians who live in that vicinity say that it was the Paiute Indians who killed the two Americans and that the Paiute live with the Utes on the north side of the San Juan River. Jesus and the Navajo who went with him say that from what they saw and heard, it is their opinion that it was the Paiute Indians who killed the two Americans." This last judgment was true, but the significance of the incident lies in illustrating the connections between the Utes, Paiutes, and Navajos in this area. News traveled quickly in those days, with visiting, trading, and political maneuverings by all three groups being a part of daily life. Also, the opportunity to pin the blame on another group was not lost, playing one against the other in order to further obscure an already confused situation.

To summarize the Navajo, Ute, and Paiute relations during the period 1860–80, the following points should be made. First, the San Juan Band Paiutes, because of friendly relations with both the Navajos and Utes, served as a bridge between these two groups who were often in conflict. In this way, strong hostilities became mellowed, and from this, cooperation grew. Second, trading, kinship, and mutual service helped to strengthen these bonds of friendship. Evidence of this involvement is found even today in the Paiutes who live in both Navajo and Ute communities, as well as the Navajos who live in Ute communities and Utes who live among Navajos. Third, because each group was considered somewhat peripheral to its main tribe's area of activity, the bonds of cooperation were strengthened so that at times a close mutual allegiance was felt at the expense of the main tribal groups. Fourth, by the 1880s those Utes, Navajos, and Paiutes living on the northern Navajo frontier were looked upon by white settlers and government officials as renegades. All through the 1880s and 1890s, whenever an incident occurred—which was frequent—the cry of "outlaw band" was raised and accusations were made against this restless group of Indians who did not come under as strict control as did their main tribes. Finally, there developed a spirit of opposition against outsiders. The drives associated with Mormon settlement, gentile mining operations, cattle companies, and general westward expansion created competition over the land and its resources. Utes, Paiutes, and Navajos living in southeastern Utah resented this encroachment and occasionally offered cover and hiding places for those fleeing from the law. Thus the bonds of friendship and kinship, forged in adversity, held these three groups together from the unrest of the 1800s into the greater tranquility of twentieth-century America.

3 / Monster Slayer Meets the Mormons on the Northern Navajo Frontier, 1870–1900

A Navajo made his way by the cold light of dawn to the top of a hill. After resting for a moment, he began to utter a prayer, using words and phrases taught him by Mormon missionaries. Before long, two spiritual beings appeared, one of whom was a large, red-bearded man. The Navajo later reported that he was counseled by these men to "give strict heed to my Mormon brethren," to tell the truth, be kind, avoid stealing, forsake war, and maintain friendship with "the superior race, the Americans." He was then "carried away in the Spirit" and saw the "earth as a Garden of Eden, a level plain; all things looked beautiful." The vision next shifted to a scene where he learned that "the Mormons and my people were living on the tops of the mountains and saw the Lord was a little angry with us all not being good and the gentiles [non-Mormons] came against us for our belief and threatened us with destruction and we were entirely surrounded by our enemies and the Indians stood up and pled for the Mormons saying they were good people." These pleas did not go unanswered; though the gentiles fired their guns, only water poured forth from the barrels, while "our Great Father" watched and laughed. Further prophetic events unfolded, taking a total of seven hours to reveal. The two beings then disappeared after showing themselves to the Navajo's wives, who saw them "standing in the air above our hut."[1]

This supernatural experience was recorded in 1881 by Christian L. Christensen, a missionary and interpreter for the Moenkopi settlement of the Little Colorado Stake of the Church of Jesus Christ of Latter-day Saints (Mormon). The vision encapsulates the fervor that at least some of the Navajos felt about their conversion to Christianity, as well as illustrating the bonds of friendship developed in Mormon-Navajo relations, at times to the exclusion of other whites. Yet perhaps the most significant point is that these feelings developed during a period of expansion, as both groups vied for agricultural and grazing lands on the Little Colorado and San Juan Rivers.

This chapter will examine the factors affecting the quality of these relationships and explain why so little friction initially resulted. Due to the scope and complexity of Mormon and Navajo expansion, the primary area of study is the two settlements of Moenkopi-Tuba City and Bluff—the former on the Little Colorado River and the latter on the San Juan. Discussion of Mormon interaction with Navajos in other areas is beyond the scope of this chapter, as are their dealings with the Hopi, Ute, Paiute, and Havasupai, although these groups were also living in this region. Similarly, this chapter will not provide a detailed catalog of towns and personalities associated with Mormon movement into this territory.[2] Instead, the primary focus is on the cultural values that affected the historical experience and the issues of expansion between 1870 and 1900.

By the 1870s the Mormons were ready for a change. The previous decade had been turbulent, with Navajos, Paiutes, and Utes raiding southern Utah to the point that some settlements were abandoned. The practical needs of survival stifled any sustained missionary efforts toward the Navajos. Forays into Indian country were made after stolen stock, not converts, while attempts to keep Navajos south of the Colorado River became a goal of many of the Utah settlements. Even the Mormons' Paiute neighbors feared the activities of Navajos, Utes, and renegade Paiutes, who continually preyed upon them. However, there were some exceptions to this general hostile resentment of the Navajo, the most notable being Jacob Hamblin.[3] But even his main interest and missionary efforts lay with the more settled Hopis to the south.

At the same time that the Navajos were busy raiding settlements, they also faced problems of their own. The 1860s saw many of them surrender to the pressures of both Indian and white attacks launched as part of a campaign to move the Navajos to Bosque Redondo in New Mexico. Those who did not surrender remained in territory peripheral to previous major Navajo activity and cautiously continued their raiding. The triangular area bordered by the Little Colorado, Colorado, and San Juan rivers, including the future locations of Bluff and Moenkopi, served as a refuge.

In 1868, the federal government released the majority of the Navajo population from confinement at Bosque Redondo to return to a reservation that included only one quarter of its original lands. A natural disregard of boundaries and a desire to utilize the surrounding territory for grazing sheep and planting crops allowed the Navajos to view their use rights in the area as a practical and desirable extension of sovereignty. By the mid 1870s, the Mormons, under the direction of Brigham Young, also started to cast their eyes south to the Little Colorado River. Yet the mounting competition for land never erupted into an armed conflict. The distrust and fear of Mormons by gentiles could have encouraged Navajo warfare, but did not. Even Mormon missionary efforts that ran contrary to Navajo beliefs proved acceptable and encouraged religious conversion of some Indians.

The first and most obvious reason for this lack of hostility was that the Navajos, and most Indian people, held a special place in Mormon religious teachings as expressed in the *Book of Mormon*.[4] This, coupled with a renewed religious fervor, encouraged individual Mormons as well as groups to re-evaluate their faith and dedication with new earnestness. The United Order, a plan of communal living and profit sharing, was one of the tools of frontier expansion used to foster close bonds in a challenging situation. Although the Order was past its period of greatest popularity in Utah, some of the Mormon settlements in the area of the Little Colorado still accepted it as an organizing principle.[5] While neither Bluff nor Moenkopi were United Order settlements, each had individuals who had practiced or at least were familiar with its goals and objectives. The period from the 1870s to mid-1880s was one of intense religious dedication for many of the Latter-day Saints in this region.

The same sort of fervor, however, when viewed in other religions, was seen as superstition. The Mormons failed to see that the Navajos had their own ways of expressing important beliefs that were central to the maintenance of their culture. Both groups had their myths—sacred stories or ways of explaining the unexplainable, which connected believers to supernatural power. Neither group had a "corner" on truth or the only "correct" lifestyle, although both thought they did.

Navajo religion is a complex, sophisticated system of beliefs that incorporates animism, animatism, and prescribed ritualized behavior. Failure to follow correct practices leads to the supernatural displeasure of the gods and subsequent consequences.[6] Central to these beliefs is the maintenance of harmony or balance between man and natural or supernatural forces. While Navajo beliefs were very different from those of the Mormons, there were also some interesting parallels.

For example, the Navajos have always seen themselves as a chosen people. According to their sacred beliefs, the gods gave them protection by allowing two boys, Monster Slayer and Born of the Water, to make the earth safe from evil incarnate. The twins' success in doing so is attested by the bodies of slain monsters (large rock formations) found throughout Navajo land. These two gods also provided the Navajos with many religious teachings, among which was that of how to stay pure from non-Navajo corruption.

Even the name *Dine* reflects the idea of being special and chosen, separate from the other "earth surface" people. If contact was made with the impure, a ceremony called the "Enemy Way" cleansed the person from corruption. The Navajos used it particularly when they came in contact with Utes or white men. The restoration of purity and harmony came through performing the ceremony, so that the individual could continue to live in a holy and sacred universe. Thus, the gods prescribed the tenets of Navajo religion and, through Navajo myths, fostered their belief of being a chosen people.

Mormons held similar beliefs. From the beginning, Joseph Smith preached the doctrine of the Mormons as a special, chosen people, a "light on the hill," and a group that God watched over as long as the members kept His commandments. Revelation after revelation in *The Doctrine and Covenants* taught this principle, so it is little wonder that the pioneers gave credit to God's influence in their lives. Brigham Young and his successor, John Taylor, sent forth settlers with a sure knowledge that they were a part of God's eternal plans in Utah and Arizona. Young encouraged this belief in his response to a letter from the newly formed settlements in Arizona: "We thank the Lord that all is well with you as it is, and we pray that your efforts to acomplish the purposes of God in the direction in which you are now called to labor may be crowned with abundant success. . . . We desire that the settlements in the Little Colorado be built up to the Lord in righteousness, wherein an example will be set to the surrounding tribes of the Lamanites, and indeed to all others of the way the Lord will build up Zion."[7] Mormons preached similar beliefs as they entered Bluff in 1880. Revelations called them to perform the honorable task of controlling the Indians and settling an area of God's kingdom on earth.

In viewing the role of God in selecting His people, one finds that Mormon beliefs functioned in much the same way that Monster Slayer and Born of the Water served the Navajos. For instance, angels and spirits visited Joseph Smith to initiate the gospel plan for the Lord's chosen. But even before these visitations took place, Christian teachings explained the role of man on earth and the basic concepts of evil and good which he must confront. Unlike the physical monsters the Navajo gods faced, the mythological heroes of Christianity fought an unseen evil. Speaking of Adam before the world was created, Mormon theology taught that he participated in a council of gods in which he helped them organize materials of the earth under Christ's direction. He was also foreordained as the first human being to wage war against Satan and his helpers who rebelled against God. This war continued on earth in the form of good versus evil and as angels opposing Satan's spirits.

The view of good and evil arising from the actions of the gods influenced the belief of the Mormons as a chosen people and as fighters against evil. One irate missionary working with the Zuni in New Mexico wrote a letter to the editor of the *Deseret News* on March 18, 1877, complaining that although his efforts to convert Indians were progressing, "the enemies of God's work have done all in their power to hedge up the way of our mission. We feel assured of success, and this because of the signs and powers of darkness raging against us."[8] Thus, Mormon efforts and activities placed in a larger, cosmological framework the powers of good pitted against evil in a divine scheme ordered by deity.

An important concept shared by both religions was that of a promised land. The Navajos felt a powerful need to have a sacred homeland, one given to them by the gods and closely associated with their mythology. The four sacred mountains—Blanca Peak, Hesperus Peak, Mount Taylor, and the San Francisco Peaks—were made by First Man and First Woman with the materials they brought from the fourth underworld. The place of emergence from this other sphere, located around the Navajo Dam area in northwestern New Mexico, was another site of holy ground. All of these locations served as powerful driving forces behind Navajo actions and beliefs. Although they were not aggressive "Zionists," the Navajos had lands designated by the gods for their use and ownership.

Because of these beliefs concerning mythological boundaries and the sacred mountains, curing ceremonies or "sings" were more powerful, travel safer, and activities blessed when performed within these bounds, while all that was outside was insecure and in the control of foreigners. A good example of the power of these beliefs occurred when General James H. Carleton urged the Navajo Manuelito to surrender and come to Bosque Redondo. The chief replied that he was not going to cause trouble but that he also believed in the traditions of his people which forbade living across the Rio Grande, San Juan, and Colorado Rivers beyond the sacred mountains.[9]

On a local level, the lands around Navajo Mountain, Utah, were also sacred for the chosen people. Buck Navajo, a practicing medicine man from this area, states that the "Blessing Way" and "Protection Way" ceremonies were performed for those who crossed the San Juan and Colorado Rivers, while the "Enemy Way" and "Evil Way" pertained to the area on the other side.[10]

This region served the Navajos as a refuge from their enemies as early as the Spanish and Mexican occupation of New Mexico. During the Kit Carson campaigns (1863–64), a severe dislocation of settlement patterns forced many Navajos into this area. It was at this time that the old mythological heroes, Monster Slayer and Born of the Water, were again called upon to protect their people. The Navajos needed a special explanation for the role of Navajo Mountain. Earlier, it had been viewed with disdain as a land to which Monster Slayer banished the ancestors of the Paiutes.[11] Now, religious justification was needed to show that this region was foreordained for the protection of the Navajos—a chosen land.

Briefly, the medicine men said that the decisive battle had already been fought before man was on the earth. A group hostile to Monster Slayer stood on the San Francisco Peaks and shot arrows at him, which today are seen in the form of tall pine trees growing on the mountain. These arrows represented the safety from harm that Monster Slayer enjoyed and so were proof to the Navajos during the 1860s, that this region also served them as an area of protection.[12] Thus the faith of the people was tied to geography. Today, Floyd Laughter affirms that "Monster Slayer did indeed catch these projectiles and plant them on this mountain. And these were designated to be medicine. They were also designated as a shield behind which we can run."[13]

Thus the four sacred mountains that supernaturally circumscribed Navajo lands remained a vital tenet in their beliefs but did not eliminate the possibilities of expansion beyond those bounds. The Four Corners region was one such area that saw continued use and increased control by the Navajo, who tied into the main body of ceremonial knowledge places and events involving supernatural beings. The San Juan River, Navajo Mountain, Monument Valley, the Bears Ears, as well as many springs, rock formations, and canyons, all held special religious significance on a local level. The four sacred mountains continued to be central to the beliefs of these Navajos, but additional places and subsequent justification allowed those living on the periphery of tribal lands to enjoy the same religious experience as those living in other parts of the Navajo domain.

The Mormons also believed in sacred lands that served as a direct link with a religious and mythological past. Although these beliefs did not promise the same type of protection and were not acted out in ceremonies, they were still an important part of Mormon teachings. According to Mormon thought, the concept of a Garden of Eden or chosen land where God and Adam (First Man) interacted was located in Jackson County, Missouri, the center of the Garden. After God expelled Adam from his presence, the exile returned to Adam-Ondhi-Ahman ("the place or land of God where Adam dwelt") and there held a great spiritual gathering.

On May 19, 1833, Joseph Smith took a group of associates to Spring Hill, Daviess County, Missouri, and pointed to a pile of rocks that had once been Adam's altar. The prophet then declared that this place was central to the Garden of Eden in the past and would be the meeting place for a great council to be presided over by Adam just before the "great and dreadful day of the Lord" occurred to usher in a millennial reign.[14] Therefore, from the very roots of Mormonism, comparisons can be made to Navajo beliefs of a chosen land.

But the idea did not stop in Jackson County, Missouri. With each successive expulsion and consequent move west, the Saints became increasingly convinced that they would find a place that God had prepared for their protection. Joseph Smith received a revelation concerning western lands as early as 1832, signifying that there was a place "appointed unto you, and it shall be called the New Jerusalem, a land of peace, a city of refuge, a place of safety for the saints of the most high God; and the glory of the Lord shall be there, and the terror of the Lord also shall be there."[15] Another prophecy given ten years later told the Mormons that they would "suffer much affliction, and would be driven to the Rocky Mountains . . . and see the Saints become a mighty People."[16] Thus the Mormon God was with His elect, guiding and directing them to the lands in which they were to live, just as the Navajos were supernaturally guided and protected in their territory.

There is little wonder that when it came time to call the Mormons from Parowan to settle along the San Juan, the Church gave the same justification used in settling Jackson County, Missouri; Far West, Missouri; Nauvoo, Illinois; and Salt Lake City, Utah: It was part of the Lord's plan, and as chosen people the Mormons participated in an important step not only in geographical but also in spiritual terms. Henry Lunt of the Parowan Stake Presidency "stated that the march of the Saints today was toward the Center Stake of Zion. . . . The colonists might very well be the first vanguard of Saints to begin the great trek eastward—back to Missouri."[17]

Lunt was not alone in his belief. Kumen Jones, an early Bluff settler, recorded in his journal that his going to the San Juan area was divinely inspired. God's will became manifest to this servant as he told his wife of a dream on December 19, 1878, just a week before being called on a scouting expedition to the Four Corners area. He related the main features of the dream as follows:

> In company with others, most of whom were strangers to me including Indians, we were busily engaged at the building of a large stone building, in which the Lamanites were deeply interested. The country was strange and new to me. Near the place of our operations was a river that I could see, the water of which was not quite clear. As this dream had left quite an impression on my mind, I asked our mother to interpret it for me, and without hesitating, she said, "You will be called with others to go and live among the Indians."[18]

Other Saints had similar feelings of obeying a divine will, as evidenced by Elder James Davis, who was warned in a dream that he would be required to go and live in the "Arizona Country."[19] Jens Nielson, leader of the San Juan settlers, voiced a firm statement of the beliefs underlying the acceptance of the mission call when he said, "It is the voice of the Lord to me to go and I am going by the help of the Almighty."[20]

Although there were many who did not want to go, and even more who did not want to stay in Bluff once the colony was settled, it was the "voice of the Lord" as expressed by Church authorities that kept them there. After some discouraging years, President George A. Smith and Apostle Erastus Snow blessed the members during one of their visits to Bluff: " 'I promise those who are willing to remain and face this difficult situation that they will be doubly blessed by the Lord.' Turning to Jens Nielson, the man added, 'For your obedient and steadfast response at this time, you shall be blessed and prospered of the Lord both in spiritual and temporal ways.' The above prophecy and promise came to pass every whit."[21]

Some Navajos even prophesied the Mormons' coming. Jacob Hamblin reported one such revelation during a conference in 1878. He said that a great change had occurred in the Indians' attitude over the preceding twenty years, at the beginning of which an unnamed Indian had received a prophecy that a "good people from the west would settle on the Little Colorado." Another Native American saw a "strange individual that had appeared to the Indians in 1875, giving them good counsel, whose name was Nephi," a *Book of Mormon* character.[22] Also, the vision introduced at the beginning of this chapter shows that the Mormons taught enough religion to the Indians for the Navajos to learn the appropriate names and forms used in Mormon prophecy.

Naturally, one of the primary tools necessary in this process was language. At first, some of the Mormons chosen for exploration and early settlement trips had to have the ability to speak Spanish, a sort of *lingua franca* in the Southwest because of previous Spanish and Mexican occupations. But before long, instructions came from Church headquarters encouraging the settlers to learn Navajo. This charge sprang from both a practical and religious need as Brigham Young pointed out that "poor, vicious or ignorant interpreters may do and no doubt have done us considerable harm and retarded us in our efforts to unite in friendly intercourse with the Indians."[23] Only a select few took this directive seriously, such men as Jacob Hamblin, James S. Brown, Thales Haskell, and Christian L. Christensen.[24] All of these men became valuable assets to their respective communities—Hamblin being a spokesman between Mormons and Navajos (though he also used Paiute interpreters), Brown bringing Navajo leaders to Salt Lake City in 1876 to air grievances to Bringham Young, Haskell smoothing over differences concerning horse stealing incidents in Bluff, and Christensen acting as the Indian Mission President for the Little Colorado Stake and often translating in church services. Mormon traders also learned the Navajo language, thus exerting an influence in economic relations, but in general, the majority of official and religious communication was handled by a small minority.

Navajos were first instructed in Church doctrine; the next step was baptism. Perhaps one of the most effective and best-recorded missionary efforts involved Christian L. Christensen. In his journal he reported that between November 3, 1879, and August 8, 1882, he baptized eight gentiles and ninety Indians. Two years later, during the month of April, he and his associates baptized forty Navajos, the average convert being twenty-four years old.[25] A normal spread of ages, ranging from eight to eighty, indicates that there was no special emphasis on baptizing children or young adults. Rather, baptism was most likely performed on families. Also, there were as many women and girls baptized as there were men and boys. And finally, according to Christensen and others, baptism was a welcomed, voluntary event.

Ammon Tenney, another missionary, tells of journeying from the Little Colorado to the area around Zuni and Fort Wingate, preaching Mormonism to the Indians that he met. On November 25, 1875, Tenney and some Navajos had a meeting which ended in a "splendid spirit and some demanding baptism but . . . being fearful of arousing the officials at [Forts] Wingate and Defiance, I declined. But so anxious were they that they appointed the day to come and be baptized at this place, a distance of twelve miles."[26]

Tenney's journal ends this episode abruptly, the next entry dated six months later, but the story does indicate the enthusiasm that some Navajos felt toward becoming members of the Church. In May, 1876, Tenney mentioned that after he had baptized thirty-eight Zunis in three days' time, twenty Navajos stepped forward to enter the water but were denied the privilege. The reason: Tenney was afraid that they did not have a clear understanding of what they were committing themselves to.[27] Thus, a generally conscientious approach to teaching clearly the responsibilities accompanying Church membership characterized Mormon proselytizing efforts.

However, Christianity had a difficult time breaking through traditional Navajo beliefs. The outward appearance of acceptance was not necessarily a conscious attempt to deceive but rather a reflection of Navajo syncretism. Because Navajo religion draws on a large pantheon of both male and female deities, the addition of one more god, in this case Christ, probably was not regarded as a really significant departure from previous beliefs.

This became most evident in the treatment of the sick, a central concern of Navajo religion. To summarize, the Navajos believed that by breaking with practices established by deity, harmony in the balance of nature or man was lost, which in turn caused natural disaster or sickness. Restoration of this balance was of utmost importance; therefore, ceremonies called "sings" were used to invoke the help of the gods. A logical step was to incorporate the Christian God, in this process especially when the normal ceremonies did not appear to have a desired effect. Thus, the Navajos took a rational approach to solving an age-old problem by joining Christ with Monster Slayer to combat sickness and death. It is in this capacity that the clearest understanding of the Navajo perception of Mormonism is found.

Some positive experiences derived from this situation. Christensen told of an eighty-year-old woman who was so sick with dropsy that she sent her daughter to bring the missionary to her. After begging for baptism, she was lifted onto a horse, taken to a river, and baptized. She emerged from the water on that cold April day, mounted her horse by herself, and went away "rejoicing," much to the relief of the missionaries.[28]

But not all who had dropsy were that fortunate, as is shown in the case of a man named Musher and his wife, both of whom were recent converts to Mormonism. In July 1886 the wife became ill, so Christensen visited the family to see if he could be of assistance. After Christensen had sat by her bedside for a short time, Musher asked the Mormon if he thought the woman would live. His answer, given in Hopi so that the attending medicine men could not understand, was that the woman would die. Apparently using another language did not fool anyone, since the "multitude present" became excited and asked the white man to explain. He reported, "I told them it was a very dangerous disease and not often cured and if she did die not to say to anyone it was witchcraft nor anything of that kind. I told them it was the judgments of God upon the earth because of wickedness and they thanked me for my talk."[29]

Christensen returned the next day and encouraged the "doctors" to let the woman sleep, something that is not necessarily part of a "sing." But "they did not dare to stop singing and making medicine on account of evil spirits." The Mormon attempted to use tact, saying that at one time the feathers, paint, and other ceremonial paraphernalia were good and came from God, but not now. They also should "sing" for free because of the "love of their sick and kindred." Turning the tables, however, the medicine men challenged him to sing for free, which he said he could not do, but that he could pray. He then

> kneeled down in the midst of them and asked God to take her away and break up their traditions and bless them with the knowledge of truth, etc. They thought my prayer was short and they asked me my opinion. I told them I thought she would die and if she did, not to tear down the house nor burn the body nor kill horses nor sheep nor goats nor dogs; that she had no need of them the other side of the vail and many other things did I tell unto them always in sighting them to their wicked practices and the necessity of abstaining from them.[30]

Leaving the group, the Mormon and Musher stepped outside for a short discussion, but the medicine men called the Navajo away because they were "suspicious" of the "privacy."

Christensen recorded a similar incident when he visited a sick member only to find "old men round him singing, buzzing, smoking." The missionary denounced the Navajo traditions, held a prayer circle, then talked and answered questions. As usual, the medicine men felt threatened and "often tried to say something to joke or confound us. But as often as they did they were confounded. I told them I had not come for fun but to do them good." The effect of this speech is questionable, but the missionary reported that in the morning after the group had been chastised by their leader, "they all went their way with very peculiar feelings."[31]

Thus, the Mormon missionaries tried to strike at the heart of the matter by denigrating traditional practices and beliefs. When one considers the complexities of cultural change and the limited exposure of Navajos to white society in general and Mormon society in particular, the amazing thing is that the Saints had as many converts as they did. Monster Slayer was far more entrenched in the fabric of Navajo society than Christ could possibly be.

In discussing historical events between 1870 and 1900 in the Little Colorado and San Juan region, one needs to look at three different groups—Mormons, gentiles, and Navajos. The Navajos, though not organized and controlled with as much clarity of purpose or economic power as the Mormons, nevertheless took an aggressive stance that in many instances proved beneficial to them. The Navajos, instead of being pawns at the white man's bidding, implemented an unofficial policy that joined armed threat, covert manipulation, legal proceedings, and practical friendship in an effective program of expansion that added to their land holdings and resulted in the eviction of the Mormons from the Tuba City-Moenkopi area.

A key to understanding why the Navajos were successful lies in Mormon-gentile relations. For instance, in 1870 the Commissioner of Indian Affairs, Ely S. Parker, received word that some white men had told Navajos there was nothing wrong with raiding Mormons, who were enemies of the United States.[32] While this misconception was corrected in a treaty signed by Jacob Hamblin on November 5, 1870, gentiles for various reasons, such as economic competition, political fear, and religious self-righteousness, continued to draw a distinction between Mormons and other whites.

One Navajo agent in particular, W. F. M. Arny, clearly exemplified this antagonistic spirit. Problems started in December 1873, when a snowstorm stranded four Navajos in Circle Valley, Utah. They had left the reservation without a pass in order to go on a trading expedition to the Paiutes and Utes. After bartering for a cow with the Utes, they took shelter in a cabin and started to dry some of the meat from the slaughtered animal. A non-Mormon named McCarty, assuming that the beef was stolen, gathered some men and then surrounded and killed three of the Navajos, the fourth escaping across the Colorado River. After a difficult journey, the wounded survivor arrived at his relatives' home and told of the deed. The Mormons were blamed, and eventually talk of war became so prevalent that Jacob Hamblin and two others went out to the Navajos' camp, where they almost lost their lives before they reached an agreement.[33]

While this story is often recounted to illustrate the peacemaking ability of Hamblin, it serves also as a good example of the complexity of Mormon, Navajo, and gentile relationships. Agent Arny sent one of his head chiefs, Ganado Mucho, to encourage peace in the Navajo Mountain area. He reported that the Indians were peaceful but that the relatives of the dead demanded compensation by the government. Arny explained that he could not pay the relatives because the Indians had lost their lives and property off the reservation, even though the treaty of 1868 allowed the Navajos to hunt and homestead on these unoccupied lands.[34]

Within a month, Hamblin wrote to Arny making clear that McCarty and his associates were not Mormons and stating that the incident could be settled if the Navajos came to the Utah settlements with a good Spanish-speaking interpreter.[35] Arny responded that Hamblin and the Navajos should come to Fort Defiance where "arrangements can be made to protect the Mormons . . . and define where such persons can settle without being molested by the two tribes (Navajos and Moquis [Hopis])." Otherwise, the agent feared, he could not "restrain my Indians."[36] The same day, Arny wrote to the Superintendent of Indian Affairs in New Mexico, Colonel L. Edwin Dudley, stating that "the Mormons are so anxious to encroach and settle upon the Moqui and Navajo lands that they are willing to pay for peace with them." After mentioning that John D. Lee of Mountain Meadow Massacre fame operated the ferry across the Colorado, Arny accused the Mormons of encouraging Indians to steal from gentiles. The agent concluded, "The Mormon leaders find that some of their followers, influenced by their zeal and cupidity, made a mistake . . . which in my judgment should be used in a peaceful way to prevent the settlement of the Mormons too near to either the Moquis or the Navajo reservation."[37]

The Navajos also wanted to use this incident to their benefit. Two chiefs, "Peoken" and "Katcheena," demanded payment from the Mormons of 192 horses, 100 cattle, and "other property" to help ease the loss of their three men. The Navajos were aware of the friction between Mormons and gentiles and capitalized on it by boasting that arms and ammunition were supplied by the "Americans" to wage war against the Mormons.[38] They made no mention of three Mormons—Dr. James Whitmore, Alexander McIntyre, and George A. Smith—killed in two separate incidents within the past ten years. In a week's time, the indemnity jumped to 400 cattle for a "deed our people never committed."[39] The Mormons sent a letter to the chiefs of the Navajo Nation encouraging a few leaders to come to the settlements, but to no avail; the Navajos played hard to get.

By May, the two-month deadline given the Mormons to pay the Navajos was fast approaching. Major William R. Price, Commander at Fort Wingate, held a council in which the Navajos agreed not to fight as long as they received corn and beef. Arny and the Navajos still insisted on blaming the trouble on the Mormons and saw the impending war—costing "hundreds and thousands of dollars"—as a natural result. To avoid this, the agent recommended that the government pay money for food to be issued and that $7,500 for train tickets to Washington be provided for ten Navajos, four of whom were close relatives of the deceased. The intent was to mollify the bereaved and give the incident a chance to quiet down.[40] Arny later filed a claim for reimbursement of $17, 364.71 for food issued to the Navajos who threatened the Mormons.[41]

The matter moved to its conclusion with Arny requesting a company of troops to go with him to Lee's Ferry for a council of peace with "Indians, Mormons and others interested." Dudley responded by telling Arny that he could not authorize the agent's leaving the reservation and that, in his opinion, Arny was not the man to bring about peaceful relations.[42] Thus the affair ended in a stalemate. The Navajos did not receive the 400 cattle from the Mormons, Arny did not go on his "essentially necessary" peace-keeping mission, and the impending war fizzled. Arny did, however, go to Washington with his Navajo delegation. The most instructive aspect of this incident is the Navajos' use of threat and manipulation to achieve their ends. Arny's fear and prejudice encouraged the course they took and provided them with the extra rations they desired.

In other cases, Mormons and Navajos worked together. Starting in September, 1875, Brigham Young gave James S. Brown the special assignment to work with the Navajos. Although his health was poor, he accepted because Young told him that the "spirit does and has dictated to me all the time to send you to take charge of a mission in that country."[43] Perhaps it was that same spirit that prompted a highly dramatic (as told by Brown) episode on the Rio Purco. As Brown and two other men traveled across the reservation, a Navajo emerged from some bushes and asked who they were. Upon hearing they were Mormons, the Indian signaled for others, to the count of 250–300, to come out of hiding and hear the "history of our forefathers." Brown related stories from the *Book of Mormon* while "tears came to the eyes of many in the audience" and others declared, "We know that what you say is true, for the traditions of our good old men who never told a lie agree with your story."[44]

This incident occurred in June 1876, and by August 15, Brown and sixteen Navajos were in Salt Lake City to meet with Brigham Young. The discussion centered on supposed wrongs suffered by the Navajos in the Little Colorado area. While the actual topics discussed were not recorded, the Navajos "made a good peace" and returned home satisfied. Brown, however, toured the Utah settlements in search of those "willing or desirous of helping to build the Kingdom of God in that region . . . and extend the curtains of Zion in that direction."[45] He lectured sixty-five times, garnered eighty volunteers, and fulfilled the prediction expressed in his letter of support from Brigham Young that "we have no fear that too many will respond."[46] Moenkopi, officially established in 1875, served as a way station for these settlers as they moved on to the Little Colorado to take up residence.

The next ten years, 1875–85, were generally peaceful and productive, encouraging Mormons and Navajos to work together. Missionary zeal, the spirit of the United Order, the isolation of the settlements, and the struggles to eke out an existence kept the Mormons humble in demeanor and dependent upon good relationships. The Navajos became the recipients of this goodwill and the objects of baptism. Their response was favorable. Lot Smith reported in 1877 that "our relations with the Lamanite continue of the most friendly nature. We, I think, will have to use caution as they are not at all backward in telling the gentiles that they do not like them and that the Mormons are their good friends. Quite a number of the Navajos keep telling us they are coming to live with us."[47]

The *Deseret News* also carried words of hope during these years, such as: "The Navajo chief Comah said he was pleased to have us come live here." "The Navajo chief Comah and the Moquis' chief Nahie having visited us sometime since, expressed their pleasure at our presence and a hope that the land would suit us. We have no fears whatever that the Indians will trouble us, believing the Lord will preserve us." "As far as my knowledge goes, all of the Navajos are pleased at our being in their midst."[48] Brigham Young and John Taylor, encouraged by this response, saw it as an answer to prayer and a fulfillment of prophecy in which "the very nature of our enemies has changed through the influences of the holy spirit; those who thirsted for our blood come bending unto our brethren desiring to know the truth."[49]

This goodwill took various forms. For instance, in March 1878, a Navajo named Pal-Chin-Clan-Na arrived in Moenkopi with news that he had fifteen Mormon horses that had been stolen from southern Utah by renegade Navajos and Paiutes. He said that he had attended the 1876 meeting in Salt Lake City with James Brown and Brigham Young and that he desired to keep the peace by living in friendship with the Mormons. He also advised that the operator of Lee's Ferry be more discriminating about letting Navajos come into Utah, since some illegally bought and sold or stole livestock.[50] Pal-Chin-Clan-Na returned the horses, was eventually baptized, and attended a Mormon temple (probably in St. George) where he received his endowments, a series of Mormon sacred ordinances.[51]

One of the most important principles of Mormon-Navajo relations was the help and instruction given in planting crops and in home industry. In advice given to new settlers in 1876, Brigham Young, counseled them to treat the Indians with kindness and to teach them to avoid gambling, warring, and stealing. He went on to say that "you, on the other hand, will give them all the encouragement, help and instruction they need to perform and improve the habit of their lives, and that your helping hands will be extended to aid them in becoming good and useful citizens of the Kingdom of the Father."[52]

This practical help to Navajo economy arrived in a variety of ways. John W. Young, Mormon leader and entrepreneur, established a woolen mill and trading post in Moenkopi in 1879. He hoped that he could capture much of the Navajo trade of raw wool and then manufacture clothing for the Mormons on the Little Colorado. Although unsuccessful and quickly abandoned, this enterprise attempted to integrate the local Navajo economy with that of the settlers.[53] Agriculture was another means of teaching and helping the Navajos. The "Minutes of the Little Colorado Stake Conference" make frequent mention of the Indians planting and harvesting crops. In August 1883, Bishop A. L. Farnsworth stated that at Moenkopi the Navajos and Hopis raised 5,000 bushels of grain.[54]

Aside from these outstanding efforts, it was most likely the daily help and interaction that fostered friendship during these years. Christensen provides a good picture of this activity. For example, in November 1883, he took 1,400 pounds of wool belonging to the Navajo Musher and hauled it from Moenkopi to Provo, Utah, where he sold it for seven cents a pound. He did this as a favor.[55] Christensen also took an old gun that Musher left in his house for months and exchanged it for a newer rifle for his Navajo friend. Musher, however, was upset at the transaction and complained until the Mormon bought him a gun similar to the one traded.[56]

Helping the sick, serving as a court of complaints, giving counsel, and feeding visitors comprised the fabric of Mormon daily life. Mormon cooperation with the Indians was so prominent that even outsiders noticed it. In an annual report, Major General John Pope commented that the Mormon "affiliations with the Navajos and other Indians are very close and intimate, and they appear in all cases to make common cause with the Indians."[57] This attitude of brotherhood, however, did not last indefinitely.

There were several causes for the deterioration of Mormon-Navajo relations beween 1885 and 1900. Among them were a decreasing interest in missionary work, an increase of economic problems culminating in the depression of the 1890s, the dissolution of the United Order by the end of the 1880s, an influx of new settlers who did not have much interest in the Navajos, and the lessening of isolation because of improved transportation facilities. But the two most prominent areas of conflict arose from gentile animosity and diminishing natural resources.

Ever since the Mormons had moved onto the banks of the Little Colorado, sharp lines of demarcation had divided them from non-Mormons. The close relationships with the Navajos bred fear of conspiracy, a common theme that accompanied Mormonism before it ever reached the Salt Lake Valley. The Mountain Meadow Massacre increased mistrust, as did other incidents—some real, some imagined—so that by the 1880s accusations about conspiracy were familiar fare. For example, in 1883, General Pope believed the Mormons encouraged the Navajos to acts of hostility and resistance and "if serious trouble with the Navajos should ever arise, there is little doubt that the Mormons will be found largely instrumental in bringing it on."[58]

A year later the Secretary of War, Robert T. Lincoln, received word that the Mormons had formed a "coalition" and that a "breakout," expected at any time, would endanger every gentile's life. In order to avoid being massacred themselves, the Mexicans and Americans planned to strike first since "law abiding citizens are tired of being run over and having their property stolen and they will resort to the shotgun as our courts are a farce where Mormons are on the jury."[59] This report came from a stock rancher, George A. McCarter, and was most likely a bid to bring pressure on the Mormons and their landholdings. Further investigation proved there was no foundation to the rumor of Mormon missionaries inciting the Navajos against the gentiles. In fact, Navajo Agent John H. Bowman said of the Mormons that "they readily acquire their [Navajo] language, use the Indians well and fairly and . . . get along better with the Indians than most gentile settlers. . . . The only objection I can see to them is their great eagerness to convert them to their own peculiar faith."[60]

One of the greatest "peculiarities" of the Mormon faith at this time was the institution of polygamy. Both Bluff and Moenkopi served as a refuge for polygamists during the 1880s, when increased pressure to stop the practice drove many into hiding. The Navajos, like the Mormons, had multiple wives and so shared similar thoughts and feelings on the subject. When Bowman sent a Navajo scout to investigate Indian activity in the Moenkopi area, he hoped also to obtain information about Mormon polygamy. The scout questioned Christensen, saying that the Navajos, like the Mormons, were counseled to keep only one wife and, like the Mormons, they did not think this was a good idea. After a long discussion about religion, the Navajo "went away rejoicing."[61]

This empathy felt by Navajos for Mormons against gentiles extended to the point where Christensen hid among Indian friends for two years before being caught by federal marshals in Bluff. At times he had difficulty restraining the Indians from shooting his pursuers.[62] Although polygamy was no longer an officially professed belief of the Mormons in 1890, the practice still continued and the stigma remained for some time to come. This was important because as problems between Mormons and Indians developed over resources, the Navajos used gentile prejudice against the Mormons to attain their ends.

Water and land were keys to survival on the Little Colorado, and as use increased and resources decreased bitter conflicts resulted. Navajos let flocks of sheep into Mormon pastures and crops, disputes arose over shares of water, accusations of theft were rampant, and cries of land monopoly prevailed. Incidents multiplied, reaching a new height in 1892 when Lot Smith, an irascible Mormon leader, returned home from his fields to find a herd of Navajo sheep in his fenced pasture. He went to his house, got a pistol, and killed two of the sheep. The Indian version of the story claims that he killed seven sheep and shot at a woman and two children who were trying to drive the animals out of the pasture. Chaehos, the apparent owner of the livestock, then began to shoot at Smith's cows, killing five of them. The Mormon next shot three times at Chaehos, who returned fire twice, mortally wounding Smith. The injured man rode a half-mile to his house, reporting "that he ought to have quit shooting when they commenced shooting his cows but he thought the Indian would not shoot."[63] When a deputy sheriff arrived from Flagstaff to arrest Chaehos, between 100 and 200 well-armed Navajos prevented his seizure. The Indians then aired their grievances, which stemmed from Mormons taking over the land little by little. Chaehos evaded capture, though for at least three years marshals and agents attempted to bring him to trial.[64] Protection by his clan members and residence in the remote Navajo Mountain region ensured his freedom.

Antagonism at Moenkopi increased instead of subsiding. A request for protection from the Navajos and Hopis was sent by Mormons to the Governor of Arizona. The Indians began to mutilate calves on the public domain. Water controlled by Mormon-built dams became an issue. And finally, word spread that the boundaries of the reservation might be extended to include Moenkopi and Tuba City.

Investigations ensued for the next eight years. Petitions and letters sent to state and federal officials did not stop the increasing number of Navajos who used the area for herding and agriculture. Thus, the burgeoning Indian population with its growing demand for lands and the conflicts with the Mormons made Moenkopi an area of contention. On January 8, 1900, an Executive Order added 1,575,369 acres of land, including Moenkopi and Tuba City, to the reservation.[65]

The expulsion of the Mormons from this area largely negated the efforts and sacrifice of earlier years. The Navajos reclaimed what had unofficially been theirs, the Hopis', and the Paiutes' before the settlers arrived, and secured it through legal proceedings in the government. The roots of the Mormons' expulsion lay in their failure to adhere to the original principles of their dealings with the Indians. While the Mormons actively sought to teach and befriend, the Navajos responded readily. However, when the settlers lost the desire to share and turned to more impersonal means, such as court proceedings and laws, then the Navajos ceased to cooperate and played against the Mormons at their own game.

Yet the real lesson of this thirty-year period is seen not in the loss but in the gain. The first fifteen years were a time of peaceful coexistence between two groups expanding their domains. The Navajos welcomed the settlers because of their forthright manner and the practical benefits of Mormon society. But the Indians never lost sight of the fact that they were a chosen people in a land protected by the gods. As the elect, they felt justified in calling upon a variety of diplomatic tools ranging from sincere friendship to overt aggression in expanding their boundaries and enriching their people. And when the land was finally theirs, probably some of the medicine men chanted a song, first used in the days of Kit Carson, to exult in their victory:

> I am spared, I am spared.
> Enemy has missed me, enemy has missed me.
> Today it did not happen, today it did not happen.[66]

4 / Navajos, Mormons, and Henry L. Mitchell: Cauldron of Conflict on the San Juan

The San Juan River winds its way through the deserts and canyon lands of southeastern Utah, presenting a challenge to those who want to use its water. Yet in the spring of 1879, for the Mormon exploring party searching for a place to settle, this river provided the only large and continuous source of water for crops and livestock. Silas S. Smith, leader of this group, was probably surprised when he ventured into the area of present-day Aneth to find a number of non-Mormon or "gentile" settlers already busy constructing houses, irrigation ditches, and a dam. The leading figure amongst these homesteaders was a man named Henry L., or "old Man," Mitchell, a character who added color and turbulence to the settling of the San Juan area.

Mitchell's importance to the study of Navajo-white relations was twofold. First, he provided a well-documented chronicle of events on this part of the northern Navajo frontier. Mitchell wrote letter after letter to Indian agents, military commanders, and other officials relating—and often exaggerating—activities of white settlers and their Indian neighbors. While Mitchell was only one of many actors in the drama that played along the San Juan, he also provided excellent insight into the function of the early trading post and problems occurring along the northern boundary, both of which will be discussed in later chapters.

Second, and more important, are the Navajos' reactions to these events. Examples of active intimidation, aggressive livestock herding, overt force, and well-aimed complaints are recorded in Mitchell's letters. These techniques were used to obtain Indian desires. Although Mitchell remains at center stage in the following narrative, the Navajo reaction to this irascible settler can be clearly observed: do only that which is desirable and aggressively defend against that which is not. The effect of this attitude can be seen in the fact that Mitchell left after seven years of hardship.

Little is known about Mitchell's early life, which began in Missouri, eventually led to Colorado, and then to Utah where he settled on the public domain—a fairly common experience for many of the pioneers in this area.[1] Prior military service is indicated by his signing a letter as a former "First Lieutenant in Company K, 8th M. S.," although he would later assume the title of captain. His son, Porter, was also enlisted in the same unit as a sergeant.[2] When and where this service was rendered is unknown, but it seems likely to have been during the Civil War, since Porter was born in 1843.[3] In 1878, the Mitchells settled into Utah with a large extended family tied together through both birth and marriage.

To unravel the genealogical relationships of this group is difficult, but it appears that in addition to Henry L. Mitchell and his wife there were at least three sons, two daughters, and three sons-in-law, each of the latter with his own trading post and farm. There were also Mitchells living in the Mancos-Cortez, Colorado, area, where Mitchell Springs gave rise to a small village called Toltec, which by 1889 had died out.[4] Yet it was "Old Man" Mitchell, patriarch and spokesman for this group, who served as the major figure in events occurring in and around his ranch at the mouth of McElmo Canyon on the San Juan River.

He arrived there in the summer of 1878, having spent the previous year in Montezuma Valley, Colorado. Like many of the settlers from this area, he traveled down McElmo Canyon, a natural passageway because of the canyon's level grade, continuously flowing creek, and excellent farm lands. By 1879, there were eighteen families, consisting of seventy men, women, and children living in McElmo and along the San Juan.[5] Mitchell selected his homestead site on one of the flood plains of the river, where he established a farm and trading post, began work on some irrigation ditches and a dam, and managed some cattle and horses. Still, eking out an existence in this area was challenging, given the fluctuations in the height of the river and the ever-present threat of Indian raids. So it was surprising to find a new influx of white neighbors coming from another direction, as Mitchell and the Mormons came face to face.

When the Mormon exploring party arrived at the Mitchell ranch, its members appeared to be welcomed guests. The Mormon group, composed of twenty-six men, two women, and eight children, seemed to feel comfortable with their established neighbors. Showing characteristic vigor, they shovelled their way into acceptance by the gentiles, by digging ditches, working on the riprap dam, and planting crops. The San Juan Stake History suggests that Mitchell's group would have given up their farming attempts if the explorers had not offered to help.[6] At the same time, groups were sent out to seek agricultural land for the future Mormon colony. Symbolically, the group showed its intent to settle by raising the American flag (made of blue and red shirts) at Montezuma Creek on the Fourth of July.[7] After two months of effort, they abandoned the dam-building project, but reached an agreement that the two Mormon families who remained behind could have a share of the crops grown by their neighbors.

On a social level, the explorers attended the wedding of Clara M. Mitchell to a Mr. Williams, the ceremony being performed by a Presbyterian minister from Mancos. There was also the assistance given to Mrs. James Davis, the wife of a member of the exploring party, by a non-Mormon midwife, who had trouble delivering the baby. While she was absent, Silas Smith approached the woman in labor and administered to her through prayer, relieving the problem and winning for Smith the epithet of "doctor" among the gentiles.[8]

This seemingly propitious start, however, was deceiving. The settlers needed help, the Mormons needed help, and both had no one else to call upon. But underlying this friendly cooperation were two different views of life. The Mormons' ideals are seen in their charge to settle this lawless region as a first step "in the march of the saints. . . towards the center stake of Zion [Missouri]," while Mitchell harbored a resentment that caused him to order his family and neighbors that "they would soon give the damn Mormon outfit the same medicine that he had assisted in giving them back in Missouri."[9] It is ironic that experiences gained in the East would be brought out to the West to meet again on the San Juan.

Before the explorers departed for Cedar City in mid-August, they constructed Fort Montezuma, about five miles below the Mitchell ranch. The James L. Davis and the Harrison H. Harriman families remained there in order to grow crops and await the arrival of the main body of Mormons.[10] They were eventually joined by William Hyde from Salt Lake City, who came as a trader to the Navajo rather than as a part of the Hole-in-the-Rock expedition.[11]

Crossing Montezuma Wash, part of the exploring party encountered one of Mitchell's sons, Ernest, and his partner James Merritt. In a previous meeting, these two had insisted they were looking for an isolated area in which they could herd cattle, but now Merritt secretly informed one of the explorers that the would-be cattlemen were really in search of a Navajo mine with ore that assayed at 90 percent silver. Desiring more company, Merritt asked the Mormon, George Hobbs, if he would like to accompany them for a quarter share of the profit—the same amount promised Mitchell. Hobbs declined because of his responsibilities to the main body of Mormons awaiting his report, but he did admit that the heavily stocked larder of these prospectors, along with the possibility of obtaining wealth, was appealing.[12] This refusal eventually proved to be a wise decision for this future settler.

In the latter part of 1879, Henry Mitchell began a trickle of correspondence that turned into a continuous stream reporting Indian depredations. In fairness to Mitchell, he was in a difficult position. His ranch bordered the Southern Ute Reservation to the east and the Navajo Reservation to the south, while to the west and north lay lands claimed by small bands of Southern Utes, Paiutes, and Navajos who were often cited in government reports as "renegades." Because of kinship ties among these groups, each used the others for protection or to shift the blame for problems away from themselves.

Real trouble started in December 1879. According to Mitchell, the Utes were off their reservation and threatening to drive the settlers from their homes. Leaders like Mariano, Red Jacket, and Narraguinip were encouraging their followers to kill cattle and provoke incidents with the settlers, in order to force them to relocate out of the Utes' territory.[13] Three weeks after this, Mitchell wrote to Governor Arthur Thomas of Utah on behalf of the "gentile" citizens of Kane County, asking the territory to supply 50 good guns and 200 rounds of ammunition for each weapon for protection against hostile Utes, Paiutes, and Navajos. This action was based on the isolated location of the McElmo settlers, the demands by the Navajos that the whites leave, and the aggressive herding of 20,000 Navajo sheep around the Mitchell household, an act which "cleared away all grass several miles back from the river."[14] The Indians' actions intensified the growing friction on their borderlands. The Navajo agent, according to Mitchell, was not in control, since he had failed to curb this activity. Mitchell then pointed out an interesting fact that remained true for several years: The Utes, Paiutes, and Navajos were friendly with the Mormons but not with the gentiles. If the guns were sent to the Ute Agent, Hiram Page, then Mitchell would see that they were put in the hands of his neighbors, half of whom were ex-soldiers and for all of whom he would be responsible. The shipment was never made.

In another letter at this same time, Mitchell placed a claim against the United States in the hope of collecting part of the Ute annuity. Stating that his earlier homestead in Montezuma Valley, Colorado, had been destroyed, he charged the government $1,000 fee as reimbursement for the two residences, a half-mile of cedar fence, two corrals, seventy acres of grain, 1,500 grape cuttings, and 2,200 peach seedlings that had been lost.[15] He, along with three other citizens placing similar claims, blamed much of this activity on Narraguinip, who was said to have admitted destroying the property because of the livestock and the fences in the area. Mitchell later filed similar claims, many of which he was accused of fabricating.

The new year brought no cessation of problems. Ernest Mitchell and James Merritt had not been heard from for sixty days. Either their mining venture was so profitable that they were too busy or else they were in trouble. The first indication that the latter was true occurred when a Navajo, Boy with Many Horses, visited a Paiute camp sixty miles above Lee's Ferry. There he saw four mules taken by Paiutes after they had killed the owners. Since the Navajo were often blamed for deeds they did not commit, they were anxious to have the affair investigated.[16] At the same time, Mitchell wrote to Galen

Eastman, the Navajo agent, saying that both the Utes and Navajos were acting "sausy" (*sic*) and that if fighting occurred, most of the settlers would be in trouble because the men were out looking for Merritt and Mitchell. However, if nothing happened in the next couple of weeks, there would be 200 men present to hold out against Indian attacks until the soldiers arrived.[17]

As February drew to a close, Mitchell's fiery rhetoric grew more urgent. Merritt and Mitchell's bodies were found in Monument Valley and Henry Mitchell went to retrieve them. Although it was a Navajo guide who led him to their corpses, no single group claimed responsibility, the Navajos blaming the Utes, the Utes blaming the Navajos, and the Paiutes serving as another possible culprit.[18]

Following the burial, Mitchell launched into some of his most vitriolic prose. Claiming that five other men had been killed (although their bodies had not been found), that the Utes were in league with the Navajos, and that both were equally bad, he went on to inform the Navajo agent, "If you can't take care of these Navajos, let me know because if nothing is done, there won't be any Navajos. In ninety days, 1000 men will be here who can kill just as well as Navajos can. These Navajos are terrors, cutthroats, thieves and murderers."[19]

Agent Galen Eastman sent out Navajo representatives to investigate the murders. They returned with word that the guilty party was comprised of renegades who were not attached to any agency.[20] A second inquiry by a Navajo and a Mexican named Jesus Alviso confirmed that three or four Indians of Ute-Paiute ancestry, living north of the San Juan, had killed the two miners.[21]

This incident illustrates how Henry L. Mitchell reacted to difficult situations. While he had ample reason to be upset and inflammatory over his son's death, the tack he took was counterproductive. First, he did not have a clear picture of events before he started making accusations. Bouncing between the possibilities of the Navajos, the Utes, and the Paiutes, he finally learned who the guilty party was—but not before offending two Indian agents and frustrating the commanding officer of Fort Lewis. Second, he resorted to threats, promising that armed action was the only solution. Third, he exaggerated events, claiming that people had been killed, who had not even been in a fight. Finally, he became the focal point for much of the written communication that came from the Four Corners area. Mitchell was a prolific writer, chronicling activities, real and imaginary, that affected interactions between Indians and whites on the San Juan. For the next five years, the Mitchell ranch, "Riverview," became an important center of Indian-white conflict.

With the arrival of the Mormons at Bluff in April 1880, Mitchell's imagination found a new field of endeavor. The Hole-in-the-Rock expedition took much longer and was far more trying than the Latter-day Saints had expected, so they stopped eighteen miles short of Montezuma Creek, their original destination, and organized the city of Bluff. Within a month, Mitchell filed a claim against the Mormons and Indians, who were supposedly driving the gentile settlers out of the McElmo and Montezuma Creek areas. Considering the bedraggled condition of the Mormons one month after their arrival, one wonders how Mitchell could write the following (original spelling reproduced):

> i have bin drove from my home on the san wan by the indians through the mormans it being no longer safe for me to live thare without protection. Tha have driven evry gentile out. The morman get the indians to do it. This is a horrible state of things. When will it stop. Colonel, i am here below Parroot City campt out and destitue of allmost everything. i have lost by those Indians several thousand dollars by the Utes and Navahoes and i think it is wright that the government sould pay me out of the indian annuity at least a part. i am getting old and wore out and then to be robd and drove from my home, i think it hard and if you can do any thing for me i will be vary great full to you.[22]

While no such conspiracy existed between Mormons and Indians to drive out the gentiles, there developed a spirit of competition between the two groups of white men for freighting business and resources. For instance, the ties between the Colorado settlers in Utah and the towns of Colorado were natural. Mancos and Durango served as depots for goods that were eventually freighted to the lower San Juan. It did not take the Mormons long to realize that although the Hole-in-the-Rock trail was an accomplishment, it was impractical to use as a shipping route to Escalante and beyond, so they also turned to freighting to and from Colorado.[23] Also, the Montezuma-Aneth area had a store, run by William Hyde, and a postal service, operated by James F. Daugherty, both of which started to rival those of Bluff.

As the Mormon community expanded, the gentiles could see their control slipping. For instance, in October 1882 a regular mail service was established from Mancos to Bluff.[24] County officials were Mormon, including judges, tax assessors, selectmen, and clerks. These Saints passed laws that reflected their interests, such as the rule that a liquor license for one year would cost 200 dollars paid in advance.[25] The Mormons also took the lead demographically, with Bluff in 1880 having 107 people and in 1890, 190. McElmo was not even included in the 1880 census and claimed only 16 people in 1890.[26]

Even attempts by Mormons to include the gentiles were unfruitful. On June 1, 1885, Henry L. Mitchell was put in charge of McElmo District Roads, but on September 7, Hyde and twelve others wanted to change the route of the county roads to go to the Colorado line via the San Juan instead of leaving the river at McElmo. Mitchell and eight others protested, perhaps because this change affected the services rendered by friends and relatives along the old route. In four months' time, the Bluff and McElmo Road Districts had been consolidated into the Bluff Road District, Parley R. Butt had been made supervisor, and the county road now went from Bluff to the Colorado state line.[27] Power politics were in the hands of the Mormons.

Meanwhile, conflicts continued with the Indians. Mitchell complained to the Secretary of the Interior that large groups of Navajos were wandering twenty to forty miles off the reservation, "robbing white men, claiming they own the land, and threatening to kill all whites. . . . I know they intend to make trouble this spring."[28] The Navajo Agent's reply to the Bureau of Indian Affairs was a handy bit of detective work. Agent D. M. Riordan began by contacting the primary Navajo leaders who lived along the San Juan, as well as the tribal chiefs—Manuelito, and Ganado Mucho—to see if any knew of an uprising. He also wrote to Mitchell and his son-in-law, James F. Daugherty, originators of the complaint, since "there is a looseness about the statements, a vagueness that gives a person really very little to work on in the way of investigation." Riordan also realized the close ties between the two authors, and though each sent a separate letter, having a different date and place of origin, the agent believed "they were written in the same house, on the same table, and (I doubt not) within the same hour," since these two men lived in the same house and were business partners. Riordan talked to more than 100 Indians, none of whom could find any proof of an incident. Finally, two close friends of the agent stayed at Mitchell's ranch for a couple of nights and observed no friction but only that "relations between the traders and the Indians seemed remarkably pleasant." The general conclusion drawn from this investigation was that the complaint was lodged in order to lay the foundation for a claim against the government in the future.[29]

Mitchell also used the Indians to protect his interests. Although he protested that the Navajos were wandering far off their reservation, he issued passes, which he had no authority to do, for the Indians to come across to the north side of the river to graze their flocks on Mormon-used public domain. "The Navajos and Pah-Utes crossed with their countless herds of sheep and goats, and from the San Juan to the Blue Mountains—north 40 miles—they eat every particle of vegetation. This caused great suffering and loss among stock belonging to the Mormons, who say that remonstrance is useless."[30] The Navajos were anxious to take advantage of this opportunity to graze flocks on the far side of the river, expanding their access to land holdings.

It was intimated that Mitchell sold ammunition and whiskey. Thus, Mitchell was able to play a number of different angles. By trying to convince the agents that Indian attacks were imminent, he prepared the way to lodge future claims against the government. The loss of property—whether real or imaginary—served as a basis for requesting financial reimbursement. Mitchell constantly insisted that troops be sent to his vicinity to provide protection; these soldiers stayed at his ranch and bought goods at the trading post. By encouraging the Indians into his general area, he added more trading business, irritated the Mormons, depleted their resources, and decreased their desire to remain.

Mitchell continually proved himself to be an opportunist par excellence. At least part of this scenario was not lost on Agent Riordan, who after explaining why the Navajos felt justified in living outside their boundaries, noted that "the Indians are persistently encouraged to leave the reservation by small traders living around through the country surrounding the reserve. These men generally treat the Indians pleasantly and the Indians listen to them. It is 'business,' pure and simple with the trader."[31]

Peter Tracy, who lived one mile below the Mitchell ranch, was not as fortunate in his relations. He had a reputation for being violent and quick-tempered, so it was a stroke of luck that he was not home when a group of Utes and Paiutes passed through his farm plot and helped themselves to corn and melons. They returned the next night, however, and Tracy demanded payment. A fracas ensued and one of the Utes, reportedly named Sore Leg from Narraguinip's band, shot him through the neck, killing him instantly.[32] Mitchell and Daugherty immediately wrote letters, accusing the Navajos as well as the Utes, though their story differs in detail from that of the investigating cavalry officer sent from Fort Lewis. They seemed to revel in stirring up trouble on the San Juan River.

But 1884 brought real trouble for Mitchell and Daugherty. Events started in February when two miners, Samuel Walcott and James McNally, left Mitchell's store to prospect for gold and silver in Indian country. Leaving behind a wagon, some papers, and personal effects, Walcott and McNally had every intention of returning to the San Juan, but after separating from the main party of miners, the two men were killed while buying supplies from some Navajos in the vicinity of Navajo Mountain.[33]

Mitchell took a personal interest in what had occurred and was able to convince Fred Fickey, an insurance adjuster from Baltimore, Maryland, and friend of Walcott, of what he believed had happened. Fickey was just as prolific in writing letters as was Mitchell, corresponding with military commanders, the Governor of Utah, and the Commissioner of Indian Affairs. Much of his information came from Mitchell and Daugherty and was tainted with their prejudices. For instance, Mitchell said that he had asked the Navajos about Walcott and McNally but the Indians became angry and attempted to start a fight. Mitchell had heroically tried to pacify them, but a fight broke out at the trading post. He next suggested that his personal letter to Fickey be published "so that the Navajo Indians will be learned a lesson."[34] Mitchell wrote a second letter, painting an even gloomier picture of the situation. Fickey relayed this information about Mitchell saying that his neighbors "are gentiles surrounded by Mormons and Indians and he says the Mormons have tried to get the Indians to kill them on more than one occasion (and I have no doubt of it). Of course the entire Mormon element and all their Indian allies will misrepresent Mitchell; they would break up his settlement if they could and will do all the lying needed to screen themselves."[35]

Fickey then went on to blame William Hyde, a Mormon and old neighbor of Mitchell's, who also had a ferry near where the two prospectors had been killed. He accused Hyde of being one of the "prime actors or originators of the affair" and was convinced that if the Indians were forced to tell the truth, blame would rest on the Mormons.[36] Nothing was further from the truth. The Mormons knew little about the incident, had no part in encouraging the Indians in acts of violence, and made very little mention of Mitchell and his following in their diaries and journals. In reality, the Mormons were busy trying to grow crops, harness the San Juan River, and maintain their own friendly relationships with the Navajos and Utes.

Now it was Mitchell's turn to have problems. On April 15, approximately two weeks after the deaths of Walcott and McNally, three men—A. Johnson, William Grove, and Victor Neff—came into the trading post, having returned from a search for the miners' bodies. While the white men were discussing their lack of success, four Navajo men and two women entered, wanting to trade. One of the Navajos took an unloaded gun and aimed it at a calf outside, then at a boy, and then at one of the white men. One of the travelers saw this last move and drew his own gun, believing he was being threatened. Another Navajo took the rifle away from the one who was pointing it and showed that it was unloaded, thus relieving tension. However, the disarmed Navajo called to his friend outside, a man named Bai-alil-le, and said, "These Americans are going to kill me." Starting towards the store, gun at the ready, Bai-alil-le threatened the white men, who drew their guns and started shooting. The first Navajo to fall was the one who had been pointing the gun in the store. Two shots killed him instantly. The sound of firing brought Mitchell's son and another man from the nearby fields; upon seeing the problem, one of them fired a shot that hit Bai-alil-le in the forehead, knocking him unconscious. The white men then rushed out of the store, firing in all directions and hitting one Indian in the elbow as he jumped a fence. Mrs. Mitchell helped the two Navajo women, trapped in the store, to escape out a back door and though they were fired upon while running, neither was hit. In the meantime, Bai-alil-le revived and escaped, as did the remaining Navajo man.[37]

In usual Mitchell style, this became an instant war, and though one cannot doubt the seriousness of the event, there also was that imaginative flair that Mitchell added to any incident. The settlers made preparations to withstand a siege by hauling water from the river, boarding the trading post windows, and sending word to the military that the "ranch was surrounded by Navajos, fight in progress."[38] Near the ranch, a group of Utes had pitched camp and had witnessed the events. Taking advantage of the action, they rode to Spencer's store four miles up the river and told the two hired men working there that a fight had broken out. Leaving the post, the two men went to

Mitchell's, thus providing a wonderful opportunity for the Utes to clean the shelves of goods, which they did. Spencer later claimed a $2,400 loss.[39]

One interesting sidelight to this action is that Edgar O. Noland, owner of the Four Corners trading post thirteen miles above Spencer's, knowingly purchased some of the stolen goods from the Utes and then wrote to the Navajo Agent D. M. Riordan, using this as "proof" that both Utes and Navajos were involved in the Mitchell fight. This led Riordan to say, "I do not see what can be expected from Indians who get their moral training from contact with such men, and there are many such."[40] Both Noland and Spencer were related to Mitchell through marriage.

That night, the Navajos returned with a large party and ran off the stock at Mitchell's post and other nearby settlements. Mitchell claimed a loss of fifty horses. Cowboys from the Carlisle Ranch, herding cattle on Blue Mountain, willingly came to the assistance of the Mitchell group, eventually swelling the ranks to a total of twenty-three people at the trading post.

Within a week, a detachment of cavalry arrived under Lieutenant J. F. Kreps from Fort Lewis. He reported that both Utes and Navajos had watched him during much of his trip, "the two tribes evidently being banded together for mischief. . . . It is the opinion here that the two tribes are assembling on the other side of the river, about seven miles distant and that the Mormons are urging them on to war. At any rate every person here is badly scared and believe what they say."[41] In reality, the Mormons had little to do with the conflict. One Navajo, named Old Peejo, warned a woman, Mrs. James Allan, to stay home and keep her children nearby because trouble with the whites was expected.[42] Platte D. Lyman, a Mormon settler, mentioned how a party of Navajos came in to trade, their main group being two days' ride back from the river. His diary then reported, "They are, as usual, very friendly to our people."[43] Also, Kumen Jones, another Mormon settler, told how he traveled to the Navajos to assure them that peace was most desirable, while at the same time allaying their fears of the cavalry.[44] There was no conspiracy on the part of the Mormons.

Short on supplies and expecting a company of cavalry from Fort Lewis and one from Fort Wingate, Lieutenant Kreps departed from the Mitchell ranch on April 27, leaving two soldiers behind to keep guard. The lieutenant was convinced that the Indians "want to kill the white gentile settlers" and that the whole affair could explode into a large-scale war.[45]

This was not true of Captain Ketchum or Captain Smith, who arrived at Mitchell's four or five days later. Both were convinced that the Indians did not want trouble, that Mitchell was the cause of the incident, and that there was no need for two companies of soldiers to be stationed there, when a squad with a noncommissioned officer would suffice. Captain Ketchum's report was illuminating: in it Mitchell claimed that he had been threatened by the Navajos because he did not give in to their demands for a better price on wool. They then threatened to kill the whites in the store, went outside and prepared their weapons, and threatened to shoot his son. "The fifteen Indians present at the 'battle' as Mr. Mitchell terms it . . . kept up a constant fire for several hours on his ranch of from two to three hundred yards range, but I failed to discover the effects of any shots upon his establishment or out buildings." Ketchum believed the reasons for animosity between white men and Indians were that Mitchell now forbade the Indians to herd sheep on the north side of the river and that "the Mitchells have not the faculty of preserving friendly relations with the Indians; three are quick tempered, especially the sons. The question naturally arises why should they have trouble with the Navajo and no other San Juan traders."[46] Captain Smith concurred with many of these findings, adding, "It is the general verdict among both whites and Indians that he [Mitchell] is a firebrand among them. I do not believe half of what he told me as there is no evidence to bear out his statements."[47]

Life did not get easier. On June 18, the San Juan River reached flood stage and washed away Mitchell's place, as well as William Hyde's and Fort Montezuma.[48] In December, Navajos came to the ranch, now established on the bank overlooking the river, to explain their need to graze flocks north of the San Juan.[49] Mitchell complained to the agent that he was being overwhelmed by the Navajos and their livestock. An investigation into the problem showed only thirteen Navajo families across the river; these were on Southern Ute land, not the public domain. The settlers living near McElmo stated that they had no complaints to make about any Navajos, but "their opinion was that Mr. Mitchell had originated the reports for his own benefit and wholly without cause."[50]

In September 1885, Mitchell was accused of withholding jewelry stripped from the body of one of the Navajos killed in the previous shooting affair. The slain man's mother and father first went to Agent Bowman and procured written permission to go and visit Mitchell, but once they reached his post, he gave them only part of the property and a promise of ten horses in exchange for the remainder. The Navajos left peacefully, going to the agent for assistance with the transaction. But as usual, Mitchell contacted the military authorities, saying the "Indians came to his house in large numbers, heavily armed and in a hostile and threatening manner; that they made threats of violence and injured his buildings, etc. [and he asked] for the presence of troops for protection." Even the Navajo Agent was attacked for the Navajo's "letter of an incendiary character." Bowman responded to Mitchell's charges with a request to the Commissioner of Indian Affairs for a letter chastising Mitchell, "who has had and makes more trouble for and with the Navajos than all of the settlers living the entire length of the San Juan River. He lies to the Indians, gives them passes, tells them that he is a brother to the Great Father, etc."[51]

Yet by the end of 1885, a change occurred. There is no further mention of Henry L. Mitchell. Indian depredations continued in 1886, 1887, and 1888, each time resulting in petitions from settlers in McElmo Canyon, but Mitchell's name is absent, although in the 1886 correspondence, Porter and Henry

F. Mitchell's names appeared. Both these men moved back to the Cortez-Mancos area, but nothing was said about their "Old Man."[52] Records of Montezuma County, Colorado, and San Juan County, Utah, are silent also. The only clue to Mitchell's departure is provided by Kumen Jones, who noted that the Mitchells spent "a very few troublesome years" in the area and then "hit the trail back out, much worse off than when they came in."[53] No doubt, this departure must have been welcomed by both the Indians and the Mormons.

In Henry L. Mitchell, one finds a quarrelsome man who rarely lacked words. Through word and deed, he was able to involve Navajos, Utes, Indian agents, Mormons, cavalry, the Governor of Utah, and the Commissioner of Indian Affairs in a series of incidents that encouraged seven years of turbulence and indecision. The Navajos and Utes responded by using intimidation and furthering their goals when practical. While Mitchell's actions at times seem inconsistent—such as his encouraging Navajos to graze their herds north of the river, then later complaining about it—he was effective in playing one group against another.

5 / Indians, Anglos, and Ungulates: Resource Competition on the San Juan

Grass, water, and trees spelled survival in the Four Corners area during the 1880s. Navajo, Ute, and Paiute groups depended on these resources because of their use in grazing herds of sheep, goats, horses, and wildlife and in providing food, medicine, and shelter. Each Native American group adapted its own cultural needs and beliefs to the environment, but all three used it intensively. For instance, the Navajo economy stressed agriculture—either by irrigation or dry farming—and the herding of large flocks of sheep. The Utes and Paiutes, on the other hand, depended more heavily on a wide-ranging quest for resources, many of which were reaped in a cyclical pattern of harvest. Deer, elk, mountain sheep, and antelope were hunted, while seeds, pinyon nuts, and berries were sought at varying elevations at different times of the year, the collecting locations ranging from the La Sal, Blue, and Sleeping Ute Mountains to the canyon floors that feed into and follow along the San Juan River.[1]

Dependence on the land was important not only for survival, but also in a religious sense. Rivers, springs, canyons, and rock formations were often tied to supernatural beings and mythological events. From the Bears Ears to the west, the La Sals to the north, Sleeping Ute to the east, and Black Mesa to the south, there were many topographical features that caused the Native Americans in this area to invest their landscape with deeply religious significance.[2]

But to the Mormon and gentile livestock owners entering southeastern Utah, southwestern Colorado, and northwestern New Mexico in the 1880s, these Indian concerns were unimportant. Settlements, cattle, money, and range lands were paramount in these white men's lives. The Mormons based their operations out of Bluff, while large cattle companies—Pittsburgh Land and Cattle, the Carlisle or Kansas and New Mexico Land and Cattle, Lacy, and Preston Nutter companies— spread their herds over large tracts of open range that stretched from the Colorado and Green Rivers in the north to the San Juan River in the south.[3] While each of these operations has been studied to some extent, little has been said about their impact upon Native Americans and the subsequent strategies to discourage the use of this area as range land. This chapter will discuss the Navajo and Ute-Paiute attempts to halt encroachment on their lands.

Mormon settlement started in the spring of 1880 at Bluff and spread to Monticello, Utah, by 1887. The initial herd of horses and cattle brought into San Juan County numbered around 1,800, and the livestock industry continued to expand, particularly after the San Juan River flooded in 1884. It was at this time that the cattle industry began to be emphasized over agricultural pursuits.[4] The Bluff Pool, a cooperative effort by the Mormons to take range from the larger gentile cattle companies and eventually to buy out their interests, was so successful that by the late 1880s many of the large outfits were gone.[5]

The Navajos' approach to the Mormon colony and public range-use was generally characterized by an aggressive-defensive policy. Although there was some cattle stealing by the Navajos, competition between the two groups was generally concerned with control of grazing lands for sheep and cattle. The Mormons settled in an area used previously by the Navajos for many years.[6] As a joint-use area for the Navajos, Utes and Paiutes, this public domain was theoretically open for exploitation by any group of people. In reality, the Mormons felt the lands belonged to them by right of settlement, so when Navajo activity brought large herds of sheep across the river, it was looked upon as an infringement of rights.[7]

In 1878, gentile settlers lodged a complaint against the Navajos and their 20,000 sheep, which for the previous ten months had ranged along the San Juan and its back country.[8] During 1881, one settler reported two Navajo herds, one of which numbered 6,000 sheep, grazing as far north as Elk Ridge.[9] In 1883, Cass Hite accused Aneth trader Henry L. Mitchell of giving passes to the Navajos to come across the river and use the Mormon-controlled range. They "crossed with their countless herds of sheep and goats, and from the San Juan to the Blue Mountains—north 40 miles—they eat every particle of vegetation . . . causing great suffering and loss among stock belonging to the Mormons."[10] Two years later, a similar letter was addressed to Navajo Agent John Bowman by twenty-three men from Bluff. The letter requested that Navajo herds of sheep and horses be removed from the north side of the river since they were "crossing in great numbers onto our stock range and doing us great damage by the way of eating up our grass and crowding our stock off of our range."[11] Thus the Navajos constantly attempted to maintain their grazing areas across the San Juan, and yet, like the Mormons, never pushed the issue to armed resistance.

Unlike the cattle companies, the Mormons initially were fixed in one or two places, were oriented along the river for agricultural purposes, and utilized the drainage system and canyons that ran into the San Juan. Thus there was not the same "sprawling effect" as found in the cattle companies. Equally important were the Mormons' efforts to project an image of peace. Families did not have the same aura of lawlessness as the cattle companies. Instead, the Navajos often came into Bluff to trade and gather what they could from the source of wealth now planted on the river. One settler wrote that as soon as the pioneers arrived in Bluff, the Navajos began friendly visits but acted as "systematic beggars and true to their instincts as Indians, they would steal small articles and everything they could get their hands to appropriating the same, for their own use."[12] Brigham Young's adage that it is easier to feed Indians than to fight them proved true for these settlers. The Mormons clearly understood the power that could be brought against them if they followed any other course of action with their Navajo neighbors.

The Navajos should also be generally commended for their efforts to maintain peace. In all the years that the Mormons lived on the border of the reservation, with its many possibilities for friction, only one man, Amasa Barton, was killed by the Navajos. There were several reasons why violence was kept to a minimum. First, the Navajos remembered their recent incarceration at Fort Sumner from 1864–68. The role of soldiers, agents, and treaty agreements had been indelibly inscribed into the tribal memory. Two incidents illustrate the Navajos' respect for law enforcement. During a dispute at the Mitchell trading post, eighteen miles above the Mormon settlements, one Navajo man was killed immediately and another fatally wounded, causing an angry stir among the Indians. The cavalry was called in to investigate while keeping the peace, but it was Kumen Jones, a Mormon settler, who visited the Navajo to ensure a cessation in hostilities. During this visit, the Indians expressed fear of the soldiers, promising that all would be done to avoid further conflict.[13]

In 1887, following the death of Mormon trader Amasa Barton, Navajos exhibited the same fearful attitude toward soldiers. Approximately 100 Indians arrived in Bluff with faces blackened and in a warlike mood. The handful of men found in the settlement were hardly equipped for war, so Bishop Jens Nielson and his interpreter, Kumen Jones, let the Navajos know that if a fight took place, the Mormons would call the soldiers in as their representatives. The Navajos emphatically replied that war was not desired, and peace arrangements were quickly made.[14]

Another positive factor in maintaining friendly relations between the Navajos and Mormons was that each group had men who made conscious efforts to avoid trouble. On the Mormon side, two of the best-known were Thales Haskell and his assistant, Kumen Jones. Having gained experience with the Navajos during the settlement of the Little Colorado area, Haskell was assigned to the San Juan mission as both interpreter and peacemaker between the two groups.[15] Jones was identified early during the Bluff experience as one who had a similar talent, and so received appropriate instruction and assignments to develop it.[16]

Of the Navajo friends, perhaps the most notable character was Jim Joe. His reputation for honesty was impeccable and appreciated on both sides of the river. One of a number of incidents will illustrate this. Approximately thirty-five miles below Bluff, in an area of rough, broken topography, there was a party of outlaws who traded Mormon cattle to Navajos and Paiutes for horses, silver, and blankets. When Jim Joe heard of this activity, he notified the Mormons, led them to the offenders, assisted in the arrest, testified in court, and helped return the stolen or traded goods to both Indians and whites.[17]

Mormon relations with the Utes were notably different from those with the Navajos. First, the Utes had a stronger claim to territory settled by the Mormons, the San Juan River generally being accepted as the dividing line between Navajo to the south and Utes to the north. The Mormon settlement at Bluff became a target for thefts, as did the herds pastured in the canyons and flats in the surrounding area.

The Paiutes and Utes in this region intermarried and depended on each other to such an extent that they were viewed as one group by both the Mormons and cattlemen. The Navajos were not far behind in fostering friendships among their Indian neighbors. The development of these ties occurred over two decades, the 1860s and 1870s. By 1881, this friendship was well-formed, so that when a group of Paiutes from the northwestern part of the reservation came to the Navajo Agency begging for food and clothes, they were recognized as associates of the Navajos who had not gone to Fort Sumner or signed the peace treaty of 1868. The Paiutes were helped "for we used to be friends and have intermarried your people with ours (that is, those Navajos who have always resided west and northwest of this reservation)."[18]

These Paiutes were primarily from the San Juan Band and had no official ties with any agency, while those of Ute ancestry who had married into the Paiute group came from the Southern Ute Agency headquartered in Ignacio, Colorado. The group formed by this amalgamation of Navajos, Utes, and Paiutes quickly acquired a reputation for being troublemakers and "renegades"—an epithet often used in government reports and correspondence.

Their reaction to the Mormon settlement was mixed. Protests against the Mormons' location were lodged because, traditionally, this Paiute-Ute (henceforth called Ute) group ranged between the La Sal and Blue Mountains in the summer and in the general vicinity of Bluff, Allen Canyon, and Cottonwood Canyon in the winter—locations at a lower elevation with less snow and more warmth.[19] But the Mormons also provided a lucrative, fixed target that was generally not aggressive. Cattle and horses were stolen, cattle were shot and left to rot, and a flow of hungry Indians demanded to be fed, all of which served as irritants to the pioneers. Writing of this period of San Juan history, Albert R. Lyman, a local historian, noted that "the Utes looked with ugly disfavor on the efforts of the colony to stock the range and though they cherished this excuse for stealing horses and eating beef, they had emphasized their feelings after every unpleasant contact, by shooting cattle and leaving them to rot on the hills."[20] The intensity and frequency of such incidents led one pioneer, referring to Navajo and Ute depredations, to say, "We are about to be crucified between two thieves."[21]

Yet the Mormon policy of peaceful coexistence seemed to pay dividends as much by what was avoided as in what occurred. During the period 1879–1923, no Mormon was killed by Utes, while the non-Mormon or gentile faction lost approximately forty people to Indian fights.[22] Two incidents illustrate that in the Indians' mind there was a difference between Mormons and gentiles. The first occurred in 1881 when the settlers went into the surrounding canyon country to reclaim eleven stolen horses. After identifying the livestock and demanding its return, the Mormons were confronted with drawn guns. Tempers flared, but no gunfight took place because one of the Utes recognized the white men, saying that they were Mormons. The horses were returned and a bloodbath avoided.[23] Once when Kumen Jones and his wife were on their way to Bluff, they met some cowboys from the Carlisle ranch. After asking if there were any Indians between there and Bluff, he was told that there were many. "Any danger in traveling the road?" "Not for your people," came the reply.[24]

The Mormons and Utes were also willing to discuss problems and reach agreements. For example, by 1887 the Mormons in their San Juan Co-op had 12,000 head of livestock, which by 1895 expanded to 20,245.[25] This growing herd, along with the gentile cattle companies located mostly around Blue Mountain and Elk Ridge, needed additional range. In 1886, the Elk or the La Sal Mountains offered good grazing country which the Mormons were able to use, through an unofficial treaty made with the Utes. Charles Peterson, who has studied carefully the development of the cattle industry in southeastern Utah, notes that "this breakthrough did not go unprotested. Indeed the Durango cowboys who had toured the Elks [Mountain] looking for grasslands in February returned in a huff, where they reported that they 'had talked with Mormon leaders at Bluff and [were] informed that they were not welcomed to locate there.' The Mormons had made a treaty with the Paiutes and one of the provisions was that no white men should locate stock in that region."[26]

Ecologically, the impact on the environment was devastating. Testimony by both settlers and Utes concerning the grazing of cattle indicates that changes in plant life, erosion of soil, and decreased productivity of grasses occurred.[27] After the Utes sold herding rights on the La Sal Mountains for $300 worth of flour, merchandise, and ponies, one settler commented that "the way that mountain was eaten up by cattle and sheep from the day of that treaty . . . probably made the old Indian's head swim and he perhaps found difficulty in recognizing it as the same verdant forest where he hunted deer and hid from pursuers."[28] This view is corroborated from the Indian's side. One Paiute summarized the problem as he told his grievances to a young white man:

> He [Posey] was somewhat concerned about preservation of the land. He told me, and Mancos Jim told me a time or two before, how the country had been when Posey was a boy. And their expression was something like the grass would grow up to the belly of the ponies. He said there was lots of grass and lots of deer and there was hunting. . . . They [cattle] ate all the grass . . . and as a result of this, there was pretty poor feed for the Indian ponies and deer. The deer population was very low, and so the Indian felt like this justified them every once in a while in killing a cow, a steer or something of that sort.[29]

But if the Mormons had problems, it was doubly true for the large cattle companies, who by 1885 were estimated to be ranging as many as 100,000 head of cattle in southeastern Utah.[30] Because of the strong Ute claim to the lands surrounding the La Sal and Blue Mountain region, the major confrontations of the cowboys were with this faction, which included Navajos and Paiutes as well. The size of this band varied from a low of 50 to a high of 200 Indians.[31] Efforts were constantly made to get the Utes and Navajos back onto their respective reservations and to keep the peace in this area, but these attempts met with only marginal success.

Unlike the Navajo-Mormon relations, the Utes and cattlemen did not have men who were actively involved in maintaining peaceful relations. Often it was just the opposite. Many of the cowboys came from a restless and ruthless background that encouraged fistfights and gun play as a way of reaching a solution to an argument.[32] The Indians would rise to the occasion, being just as quick to anger and to provide reasons for a fight. Two of the more important such incidents were the Pinhook Draw fight in 1881, which started with a shooting at a line cabin and ended with thirteen cowboys and gentile settlers killed, and the White Canyon fight in 1884, involving a posse of cowboys and the cavalry from Fort Lewis, with two men killed.[33]

Most incidents occurred on a small scale, usually when the Indians caught one or two white men isolated and vulnerable. Often the Utes were in the act of taking the stock or already had it in their possession, and the cowboys would attempt to take it back. This pattern was repeated numerous times—the incident that provoked the White Canyon fight is a good example. Problems started when some white men recognized a group of Utes with four cowboy horses; when the white men went to retrieve them, one of the men was sliced in the neck by an Indian's knife, after which the cowboy planted two shots in the Ute's chest. A general fight ensued with two cowboys wounded, their horses stolen, and their wagons and supplies captured.[34]

Another example of this small-scale violence involved Henry Hopkins, a cook for one of the cattle outfits. Left alone in camp, Hopkins was later found dead—shot in the back, presumably by Utes. Harold Carlisle, the English cattle baron, wrote to Ute Agent Charles F. Stollsteimer, placing the blame on the Indians, who "display a perfect arsenal of the most improved weapons and ammunition." Perhaps part of Carlisle's fear also stemmed from a member of this band: "a murderer from Leavenworth jail [who] has openly boasted of his intention to kill myself and my wife."[35] The guilty party was never found, but a subsequent investigation noted that the Indians were not opposed to peace, but that the murder of a Ute family by cowboys two years before had created apprehension on both sides. Perhaps this is why a Mormon was the first to be notified by the Indians about Hopkins's death. Within two weeks' time, a company of soldiers was stationed in the Blue Mountain area to maintain peace and encourage the Indians to move back to their reservations.[36]

Keeping the Navajos and Utes on their reservations was another story. By the mid 1880s, the Navajo agent became increasingly upset by the Utes from the Blue Mountain region because they were "a bad element to have among our people and we do not want them with us."[37] Correspondence exchanged between agents at times became heated, but the general tenor of thought is summarized in John Bowman's letter to the Southern Ute Agency. He pointed out that the Navajos were willing to receive friendly visits from the Utes "but they [the Navajos] are not willing that these renegades, cut throats and thieves should make this reservation their place of refuge. . . . We are not willing to entertain the renegade Utes and do not want you to receive the renegade Navajos."[38]

In spite of the agent's wishes, friendly exchanges between both renegade and peaceful Indians continued. Even into the 1890s encouragement was given to Navajos to join the Utes in depredations against the cattle companies. One rancher living in Utah along the San Juan River wrote that

> there is a large number of Navajos from their reserve in Arizona, now on the Mancos and Mariano [a Southern Ute] is inviting more to come over. I saw him a day or two ago and I told him that you said for the Navajos to stay on their own ground. Mariano claims to own all of San Juan County and it is bad enough to have him and his outfit living off the cattle herds without his inviting a lot of Navajos to help him out. The Navajos have killed two cowboys up at the Hogback Mountain recently and I would not be surprised if things were not pretty lively on the San Juan in the spring.[39]

Besides killing cattle and fighting cowboys, this renegade band also used fire to scatter the herds of livestock and to drive them from the range lands. Perhaps the burnings served a second function of ridding an area of brush and fostering better grass for Indian animals. But to the cattlemen this was just another form of harassment. Edmund Carlisle complained to the Ute agent that the Indians were killing cattle and burning grass and timber to such an extent that "unless something is done to check them, they will do very serious damage. The citizens talk of organizing and killing off these Utes."[40]

Similar letters were sent by other ranchers in 1882 and 1884, and matters seemed serious enough to send Special Indian Agent John F. Tapping to the Blue Mountain region to investigate.[41] There he found more than twenty cows shot and skinned and the carcasses partly burned, while the area south and west of the mountain had been torched—reportedly by Utes.[42] The effectiveness of the Indians' tactics was also discussed, Carlisle indicating that in June and July 1884 his company had lost 150 horses, 750 cattle, and a number of wagons with supplies taken by the Indians during fights. A claim for losses accompanied these figures.[43]

To suggest that the Utes were acting out of blind rage to counter the cattlemen's encroachment is not entirely true. The Indians understood clearly what needed to be done in order to maintain a viable economic position and to get what they wanted. John Bowman, the Navajo agent during the mid-1880s when the Utes were at their militant height, very accurately described what was happening. He wrote:

> If the Navajos were not the best-natured Indians on the continent they would cause lots of trouble for they are continually told by their Ute neighbors on the north as well as by the Apaches on the south, that the only way to get any help from the United States is to go on the warpath and then be hired to quit. . . . The Ute says, "We killed our agent and one belonging to the Navajos; we have kept the good people of Colorado, as well as others, in dread for years. Come over and see them pay us, our wives and babies, a good many dollars in cash each year, just because they are afraid of us. Go and kill a few women and children; then you will be noticed and remembered; 'Uncle Sam' has forgotten you." It is hard for a poor Indian who has never seen much of this world to understand why the distinction is made and I am frank to confess that it puzzles me to know why it is so. The treaty stipulations, conditions, reservations, and all other things are exactly similar, only that the Navajos are industrious and peaceable and the others are not.[44]

The Utes proved quite adequately that the squeaky wheel does get the grease.

However, not all the blame for problems can be placed on the Indians. Both Navajos and Utes had grievances that were identified by their agents. For the Navajo there was an uncertainty of the boundary so that "stockmen generally assume that the reservation line is where their interests or wishes may dictate." Also scarcity of water forced the herds onto public lands, which the Indians had as much legal right to use as their white neighbors. A treaty clause permitted hunting on lands adjacent to the reservation, which often irritated the settlers, and finally, small traders encouraged Indians into their areas on the periphery of the reservation to increase business.[45]

One example of traders' activity involved a tussle between Harold Carlisle and some Navajos who were ranging livestock in the Gallegos Canyon area of northwestern New Mexico. The Navajos accused the Englishman of running off their animals and herding his cattle on the reservation. On April 22, 1884, four Navajos approached Carlisle and his men and started a scuffle. One of the Indians picked up a lead pipe; Carlisle drew his revolver, cocked it, and backed away from his opponent. Tripping over his spur, Carlisle fell backwards and fired his gun into the air, encouraging the Navajos to disperse. When an officer investigated the affair, he found that behind the incident stood a trader, whom he suspected provided liquor to the Indians, encouraged confrontation, and stirred up anger, in order to maintain his customers.[46]

The Utes also had their own series of problems. According to one of the white men living six miles north of the Southern Ute Reservation, there were many settlers dwelling on both sides of the boundary line so that they could graze hundreds of cattle on Indian grass. There was also a group of lawless white men who burned cabins and stole horses so that the range would remain unsettled and unfenced for the cattle industry. The blame was put on the Utes. For the same reason, cattlemen preferred the Indians over the settlers, since the Indians were easier to manipulate. Removal of the Southern Utes would have been detrimental to control of the grazing areas. Liquor sales were yet another problem.[47]

Cattlemen were not the only invaders. For almost a year, Southern Utes complained about two men, Dod O'Connell and J. Benedict Martinez, who grazed 26,000 sheep on the southern slopes of Sleeping Ute Mountain. The Indians complained that if nothing was done about these infringements, they would move off the reservation, taking their herds elsewhere.[48] Although this did not directly affect the renegade Ute band of the Blue Mountain area, this incident helps illustrate why Southern Utes left the reservation and willingly joined them in depredations against white stockmen.

The law was often turned to the advantage of the cattle owners. Claims against the government were submitted in hopes that payment would be made from the Indians' annuities. One such attempt made by the firm of Willis and Flemming gives an idea of how exaggerated these claims became. In 1881, the Ute agent received a complaint against the "Utes, Paiutes and renegade Navajos" who damaged the herd of Willis and Flemming to the tune of $9,909. After an extensive investigation, the agent determined that: (1) most of the claim was based on hearsay; (2) the lost cattle were badly overpriced (they were worth $1,600 at the most); (3) only eight head were lost; (4) Willis was killed seventy miles from his cattle range while bent on avenging the death of a friend; and (5) 300 sheep and goats had been taken from the Indians. The investigator recommended no payment of loss to the firm.[49]

The law was also manipulated on behalf of the cowboys in court. On December 26, 1889, a Navajo man named Chiz-Chilla [Chishchili or "Curly Head"], two women, and a boy were hunting deer in San Juan County, New Mexico. A group of ten or twelve cowboys entered the Indians' camp and stole some property, among which was a blanket. Chiz-Chilla pursued the thieves and received his blanket back, but not before the two parties exchanged hot words. The next day the cowboys met him on a trail, he fled, and, after his horse slipped, he dropped his rifle which accidentally misfired. The cowboys dismounted and took up firing positions, shooting until they killed the Navajo. The main leader of the group, John Cox, and his friends entered town and "swaggered around like heroes." An investigation ensued with the promise of a grand jury to be held in Aztec, New Mexico, in May. The cowboys first tried to buy their way out of trouble by offering $200 in payment, but Chiz-Chilla's family refused to take it, insisting on a trial. The Navajo agent was assured by both the sheriff and the prosecuting attorney that he would be contacted as soon as a date for court was set. This was never done. Cox went to trial, presented only his side of the case and was found not guilty. The grand jury was composed of cattlemen, and the sheriff was a cattleman who depended on cattlemen for reelection. The Indians were indignant at the turn of events, especially as they remembered that a Navajo had recently been sentenced to a long term of imprisonment for a similar deed. The agent found himself doing some fast explaining while handing out stoves, shovels, and harnesses to the Indians to appease them until a new trial date could be set.[50] No record exists, however, of any further judicial proceedings.

One final consideration in understanding the competition for resources in the 1880s and 1890s revolves around the issue of game animals, particularly deer. Almost every year during this period, citizens wrote letters of protest concerning the uncontrolled slaughter of deer by the Indians. There were a variety of reasons why these hunting practices occurred, but the main one was for hides. One person suggested that the Indians "saw the handwriting on the wall and knew that they were going to lose southeastern Utah to the whites so decided to kill all deer possible for the hides then drive the balance as near as possible towards their reservation."[51] Complaints of illegal hunting and slaughter of game, however, continued to be sent to government officials into the 1930s, long after the Utes and Navajos had well-established reservations and were no longer dependent on game.

Perhaps a more satisfying answer rests in the development of a trading post system, both on and off the reservation, that increased the possibility of obtaining more of the desirable white man's goods in exchange for hides.[52] Credibility is given to this interpretation by a cavalry officer who visited the Blue Mountain area in December 1889. He wrote:

> The Indians have this fall killed a good many deer, as is shown by the number of hides they have sold to the trader. Whether

> or not they have killed deer solely for the hide cannot be ascertained unless the statements of the people of that vicinity are accepted. . . . [They] say the Ute Indians use the meat of the deer killed while the Navajos leave the carcass and kill for the hides alone. The trader at Monticello, Mons Peterson, concurs in this opinion and says that the Navajo Indians sell a great many more green hides than the Utes; that they kill more deer either because they are better hunters or because they have so much better horses. The number of deer said to be killed for the hides is probably exaggerated.[53]

If the number was exaggerated, it continued to be so in the years to come.

Native Americans often deny this type of report, saying that it is false and is used to debunk the ideal of Indians living close to the earth. Examples of intense, ritualistic behavior—especially by the Navajos when deer hunting—is also used to counter this line of reasoning.[54] And yet in Walter Dyk's *A Navajo Autobiography*, Old Mexican tells about a hunting expedition conducted in 1890 in the Blue Mountain area, where he remained for thirty-three days and killed seventy bucks and does. Three days later he went again, hunting only for the skins and killing sixty-seven deer, valued at fifty cents a hide.[55] If this had been an isolated incident, then perhaps the impact on the deer herd might not have been significant. If one relies on reports, however, it was a frequent occurrence.

The Utes, who did not have large flocks of sheep to depend on as did the Navajos, exerted even heavier hunting pressures. Reports vary as to the numbers of deer killed but excerpts from letters of the time indicate at least the white man's perception of what was taking place. In 1886 the Utes were said to have killed on the La Sal Mountains "several thousand deer simply for their hides."[56] A letter in 1887 reported that "about a month ago about eighty Utes went north of here [Cortez, Colorado] into the mountains and according to their own story, killed at least 200 deer, among the lot numerous fawns. The skins of the latter do not bring them twenty-five cents each."[57] Again, in 1892 a Colorado newspaper indicated that "they [the Utes] had already made one drive or roundup and had killed seven head of elk and thirty deer. It is presumed that the Indians are simply after the hides as the carcasses are left to rot and fester in the sun."[58]

White people were irate at such slaughter. Writing petitions to A. L. Thomas, Governor of Utah, the "Citizens of Grand and San Juan Counties" complained that the "Blue Mountains are overrun by stragglers and bands of Ute Indians . . . who are committing serious depredations and damages . . . killing game for the hides alone." The petition had 107 signatures.[59]

State Fish and Game officers also got involved, demanding to know what right the Indians had to break game laws by hunting out of season and killing does and fawns. "The complaint is so general that something must be done to prevent the annual recurrence of this wholesale slaughter by Utes of our game in violation of law."[60] But as one agent pointed out, it would be impossible to keep the Indians on the reservation unless a cordon of soldiers was placed "around every reservation to keep the Indians in and the whites out."[61] As late as 1935, complaints were registered concerning Navajos and Utes staging drives for deer.[62]

A final point needs to be made concerning competition for deer between Native American groups. The Navajos and Utes appear to have stayed to themselves when hunting. There was alarm, however, when large bands of Utes and Navajos were on the Blue Mountain hunting at the same time. "The two bands getting into a quarrel between themselves and fighting might make it dangerous for whites."[63] No such incident has been found.

Conflict between the Southern Utes of Colorado and the Ute-Paiute group from Utah occurred on at least one occasion. Hatch, a leader of the Paiute faction, was camped with "Cowboy" and some Southern Utes. Discussion about the deer on the La Sal Mountains excited the two men, the Paiute wanting to protect the herd while the Ute wanted to drive the deer over onto his reservation. Guns were drawn, and Hatch was shot and killed, the two camps then separating.[64] An Army report, filed shortly after this event, mentions a group of Paiutes entering the town of Monticello from one end, some Utes entering from the other end, and both groups being taken by surprise by the others' presence. The Indians dismounted and prepared for battle around the Mormon houses, until the whites were able to persuade both groups to leave peacefully.[65]

In summarizing events and attitudes of the 1880s, it is important to realize the tremendous influx of people with different lifestyles that was occurring at this time. Mormon and gentile settlers, cattlemen and sheepherders, Navajos and Utes, all played a role in adapting their ways of life and expectations to a turbulent era of history. The success that the groups achieved or failed to achieve depended on their flexibility to adapt and their ability to protect what they deemed theirs.

For instance, it was to the benefit of the Navajos generally to avoid armed conflict and instead to rely on using their large herds to put pressure on grazing lands. This approach placed the settlers and the cattlemen on the defensive without creating a need for military intervention. The Utes, on the other hand, did not have large herds of sheep, and their territory was frequently encroached upon. Accordingly, they chose to use armed resistance as the most effective means to stop their opponents. The Mormons, because of their pacific policy towards the Indians, avoided fighting the Utes and Paiutes but still had their livestock killed. So it was the cattle companies who took the brunt of Ute aggression, which intensified because of the diminishing herds of deer, the overgrazing of the range, and the inadequacy of reservation boundaries. Yet no matter what tactics were used by any of these groups, they were all eventually subsumed in the greater press of change wrought by the closing of the public domain and the end of the American frontier.

Located in Butler Wash and constructed in the mid to late 1800s, this "male" hogan is one of the few early Navajo dwellings in the north still standing. The earliest remains of hogans in southeastern Utah have been dated to 1620. (Laura Casjens, Utah Museum of Natural History)

Ute warriors were noted for their tracking and fighting abilities, which were used against the Navajos during the 1860s. Isolated dwellings, small population density, and a predictable lifestyle made the Navajos a ready target. (H. S. Poley, Denver Public Library, Western History Collection)

Navajo Mountain became a refuge for scattered Navajo bands fleeing from enemy pressure during the "Fearing Time," the era of the Long Walk. The mountain's isolation, deep canyons, and multiple sources of water allowed horticulture (note garden in foreground) and livestock herding to continue. (Robert S. McPherson)

Hashkeneinii, photographed here in 1909, found refuge at Navajo Mountain during the 1860s. He earned his name "Giving Out Anger" during his desperate flight with family and friends to safety. (Cline Library, Northern Arizona University, Stewart Malcolm Collection)

John and Louisa Wetherill's trading post, located in Kayenta, was built in 1910 to capture the flow of traffic through Marsh Pass in northern Arizona. As at their earlier posts, here the Wetherills depended on good customer relations and on obtaining Navajo products that sold in the national economy. (Used by permission, Utah State Historical Society, all rights reserved; O. C. Hansen Collection)

Holley's trading post in Aneth, shown here in about 1900, was a focal point for Navajo economic, governmental, and social activity in this part of the reservation. The structure, though modified, is still one of the oldest operating businesses in southeastern Utah. (Denver Public Library, Western History Collection)

Navajo entrepreneurs moved about in search of lucrative markets. The handwritten caption on this picture states: "Navajo Indians exhibiting their blankets and offering same for sale at 'Holley's' trading store near Bluff City, Utah." (Denver Public Library, Western History Collection)

The blankets displayed by these weavers at the same "fair" near Holley's show the varied designs available at the turn of the century. (Denver Public Library, Western History Collection)

Jim Joe, an advocate of peaceful relations, worked hard during troubled times as a mediator between Navajos and Mormon settlers. On more than one occasion, he testified as part of court proceedings in Salt Lake City. (Denver Public Library, Western History Collection)

Christian Lingo Christensen, who was appropriately named, considering his characteristic missionary zeal, spoke several languages and was a staunch advocate of Mormon beliefs. His faith and friendship brought many Navajos and Paiutes to Christianity. (San Juan County Historical Commission)

This family was photographed outside their "female" hogan near Bluff in the early 1900s. This was a typical Navajo residence of the period. Facing east and built with a cribbed roof, a home such as this one, made of cottonwood logs and covered with dirt, was warm in the winter and cool in the summer. (Denver Public Library, Western History Collection)

William T. Shelton, founder of the Shiprock Agency in 1903, was liked, respected, and at times feared by Navajos in the region. He enforced laws and was not averse to using Navajo police as well as the military when he deemed it necessary. Here he is flanked by soldiers who helped arrest some Navajos at odds with his policy. (San Juan County Historical Commission)

6 / Boats, Booze, and Barter: Trade on the Northern Navajo Frontier, 1870–1910

The trading post as a part of Native American economics has been a long-standing institution, dating back to the early 1600s. Both troublesome and helpful, traders required continuous regulation by the government because of their frequent interaction with Indians. This was particularly true by the 1870s, as organized trade grew in economic importance to the Navajos, who were now established on a reservation and started on the road to "civilization."

On the northern Navajo frontier, however, agency control from Fort Defiance was sporadic and often after-the-fact, creating an open season for white entrepreneurs seeking trade opportunities. Mormon and gentile, settler and itinerant, scoundrel and saint descended upon the area stretching from the San Juan to the Little Colorado River to ply their trade with Utes, Paiutes, and Navajos. The result: a period that started in chaos but ended in a semblance of order, making possible the golden years of the trading posts in the early 1900s.[1]

As mentioned previously, the Navajos viewed the San Juan River as their boundary with the Utes, a belief that had mythological as well as historical origins. Although most of the river did not become an official border of the reservation until 1884, it was still a landmark used by the Navajos to delineate their territory. And it was to this border that traders came to do business. As early as 1870, the agent received word that a man named Charley was frequenting the northern part of the reservation to trade goods, especially arms and ammunition, in exchange for livestock stolen from the Mormon settlements in southwestern Utah. He then drove the horses and cattle to Albuquerque and sold them.[2] Official records do not indicate that Charley was caught. Others soon joined the trade in arms and ammunition.

This was especially true as increasing numbers of settlers moved onto the public domain and started to hem the Utes and Navajos into their prescribed reservations. Troubles resulted that provoked fears of armed resistance; the Navajo agent in 1876 received word that Utes were in the Chusca Valley encouraging the Navajos to buy as much gunpowder and lead as they could in preparation to wage a war against the encroaching whites. The agent then expressed a sentiment that would serve as a recurring theme for the next thirty years—the desire for control of the off-reservation trader. After saying he realized that recent legislation had been passed concerning Indian trade, the agent pointed out that the act needed to be more stringent when dealing with the sale of arms and ammunition

> for if I understand it rightly, it applies to Indian traders and not to any citizen who may see proper to trade with the Indians. Upon this reservation there is [only] one licensed trader. . . . Anyone can establish a trading post within a quarter of a mile and be outside of the control of the agent. And one party who has such a trading post informed me that he preferred to have his store outside of the reservation, for the reason that one could not prevent his trading with the Indians and getting such prices as he pleased.[3]

When this is contrasted with what was desired by the Indian Office in its "Rules and Regulations" dated August 15, 1876, it is apparent why so many traders stayed off the reservation. For instance, the applicant seeking a license (1) had to be of "unexceptionable character"; (2) could not have had a license revoked; (3) needed letters of reference or to be known to the Commissioner of Indian Affairs or Indian agent; (4) had to be bonded at $10,000; (5) was required to provide the agent with invoices and bills of lading to check prices; and (6) was permitted to sell only goods "as may be approved by the Commissioner of Indian Affairs and at prices he shall fix from time to time."[4] In addition, no alcohol could be sold, while arms and ammunition were to be traded only in limited quantities by special permit. Thus, instead of encouraging cooperation, tight control in a frontier setting drove prospective traders to the fringes of the reservation to reap their profits.

Navajo customers were not long in crossing the San Juan. Selling staples such as flour, sugar, salt, coffee, and tools, the traders bought raw wool, woven blankets, silver, and livestock, all of which were shipped to the railhead at Alamosa or Durango.[5] Also, many Navajos had already crossed the river to graze their sheep on the public domain and to hunt in the La Sal and Blue Mountains. The trader had only to offer desirable goods, and a line of customers appeared at his counters. D. M. Riordan, a Navajo agent, complained in 1883 that "the Indians are persistently encouraged to leave the reservation by the small traders living around through the country surrounding the reserve. These men generally treat the Indians pleasantly and the Indians listen to them. It is 'business' pure and simple with the trader."[6]

Estimating the number of settler-traders who decided to supplement their income with Navajo silver, hides, wool, and blankets is difficult. The period between 1880 and 1900 saw a great deal of turmoil caused by Indian warfare, boundary changes, grazing disputes, mining strikes, poor farming conditions, and problems in legal jurisdiction. The list of new and defunct trading posts shifted with the times, but to give a rough idea of numbers, in an approximately thirty-five-mile stretch along the San Juan from below Bluff, Utah, to where the Four Corners meet, records indicate at least seven stores operated in 1885.[7] Another section of river heavily endowed with traders was the Aztec-Farmington-Jewett area, where farmers and townspeople opened posts to serve the Navajos and Utes. One trader from this location complained that on "the north bank of the San Juan River every few miles there is a trading store which depends on the Navajo for support."[8]

Yet the increased demand for trade and subsequent increase in contact also brought an escalation of conflict. Take, for instance, the seemingly harmless ferry that brought customers from the south side of the river to the north side. Many of the posts had them, since each store was usually located in a strategic crossing place to capture a natural flow of traffic. The posts owned and operated the boats with the idea of alleviating the barrier of the river and depositing the customers at the store's front door. This practice was in direct defiance of the Navajo agents, who attempted to control trade. The posts also indirectly encouraged more conflict by wooing the Navajo off their reservation and into the arms of unscrupulous traders, gamblers, and settlers.

The plight of Agent E. H. Plummer in 1893 gives an interesting view of problems associated with ferries and trade. The initial spark occurred on April 5, at the store of James F. and William W. Daugherty, the former having already spent a turbulent six years on the San Juan. The ferry, which ran on a cable across the river, was commandeered by two Navajos who wanted to take it to the south shore. William Daugherty feared the boat would be swamped through mismanagement and so called for the Navajos to come back. They refused. He then fired two shots in front of the craft, forcing them to return, but in a short while they reappeared with a group of thirty warriors to back up their demand for $200 in exchange for not burning the Daugherty store. Since the five white men at the post were heavily outnumbered, they paid the money and sent for the agent. A few days later one of the Navajos, encouraged by some alcohol, decided to burn the crib that supported the cable on the far bank and then threatened to kill William Hyde. By the time Plummer arrived, tempers were heated on both sides so that only the threat of cavalry calmed the Navajos. Eventually the two guilty Indians surrendered and went to Fort Defiance to stand trial in the tribal Court of Indian Offense.[9]

The incident prompted a series of letters between Plummer and the Commissioner of Indian Affairs that brings into focus the controversy surrounding trading posts on the San Juan. The agent pointed out that the ferries were used to haul wool across the river, serving as magnets to the Indian population. He recommended that ferries run by trading posts either be licensed or forbidden to operate, depending on the owner's reliability. Those licensed posts would carry government goods sold at cost plus transportation and clerk hire; the wool, hides, and so forth bought from the Indians would be sold by the agent or clerk in charge; and the traders who carried $3,000 worth of goods would be bonded at $10,000 and receive a salary of $2,000 per year. This plan, therefore, allowed substantial savings for the Indians.[10]

Acting Indian Commissioner M. Armstrong did not like the idea. He felt that the ferries were not detrimental to peace and the Navajos' welfare because the Indians should have "the widest latitude in bartering and trading" and should be able to bring their produce and articles to the nearest town to sell. Plummer responded that he was not suggesting the Navajos' freedom be curtailed, but that he wanted to foster the development of "responsible, reliable, worthy traders" and avoid the "unlicensed, unlimited and unregulated" commerce that encouraged "illegal traffic, too much freedom to unauthorized roaming over the country north of the river for illegitimate purposes, ready access to gamblers who infest the north bank of the river at this season of the year, when the Indians have money from the sale of wool or other products." Plummer then explained that he knew of Indians who left the reservation with money, pony, rifle, and goods but returned shortly afterward with only a gee string, having fallen into the clutches of the professional gambler. He concluded by saying:

> The theory of Indians having the widest latitude in bartering and trading is excellent or would be if all traders were honest or the Indians competent to protect themselves and understand their rights in trading. But where a trader offers a drink of intoxicating liquor for every sack of wool brought to his store or allows his ferry to be used for transporting liquor, while blankets worth from ten to forty dollars are bought by traders for from two to ten dollars; silver belts worth fifty dollars pawned for fifteen to twenty dollars are sold when opportunity offers; while the reservation is surrounded by traders and gamblers who are reaping profits of thousands of dollars annually at the expense of poor, half starving, ignorant Indians, I must continue to believe that a somewhat more limited regulated freedom in trading facilities would be more beneficial.[11]

Thus the agent had a far different and probably more realistic perception of the problem than did the Commissioner in Washington.

At least one licensed trader, H. C. Adams of Fruitland, New Mexico, agreed with Plummer's views. After complaining about the incessant roaming of the Navajos, the "tin horn gamblers who rob with impunity," the whiskey sales that led to depredations, and the lawless element in the border towns, he pointed his finger at the trading posts and ferries that encouraged this type of activity "for the illegal purpose of taking the Indians from the reservation." He believed them indirectly responsible for the damage done by Navajos north of the river and, in particular, for the death of a trader named Welsh. Adams closed his letter by encouraging the Indian Department to take strong measures against the ferries and trading posts along the river.[12] Ironically, six months later Adams lost his footing on his own ferry and drowned in the San Juan, leaving a store full of pawn to be redeemed by his Navajo customers.[13]

Yet these problems were not just those of the Indian agents; the traders had some difficulties too. With Navajos roaming off the reservation during the 1880s and 90s, there was apt to be trouble, and while the posts were not the only reason for the Indians to travel, they were a contributing factor. An estimated 10,000 Navajos were beyond the reservation boundaries in just one year.[14]

In 1886, James F. Daugherty, trader and postmaster in Riverview (Aneth), Utah, complained of Navajos and Utes wandering over settlers' property, taking livestock and creating a nuisance.[15] A little over a year later, he and eighteen other "Citizens of McElmo [Canyon]" sent a protest about Navajos stealing horses and then selling them back to the settlers at five dollars a piece. The petition had signatures of at least seven traders.[16] Eight months later, Daugherty again complained that he had lost twenty-three horses and had received none of them back and that since his arrival in 1880 there had been at least six white men killed and no punishment given to the Navajo. This was one factor that encouraged the two Daugherty brothers to withdraw from their trading post in July 1893.[17]

They were not alone; many of the traders faced severe problems during the 1890s, as part of the general economic depression throughout the United States. There were also other factors, such as extremes in weather creating poor harvests, overproduction of wool blankets, and valuables pawned to such an extent that little was left to exchange. The Indians were starving, unemployed, and calling on the government for assistance, so the traders did the only logical thing—withdrew from their business and went on to other endeavors.[18] By 1895, only the Four Corners Trading Post, owned by Owen E. Noland, was still in operation, the others having closed down, and even Noland did little bartering because the Navajos had little to sell.[19] The trading business revived a few years later as the economy improved, but for many of the old traders in the peripheral areas the slump was too much to handle and they remained out of the business.

Another problem that has often been connected with the Indian trade and white men was liquor—and the northern Navajo frontier in the last decades of the nineteenth century was no exception. Starting in 1877 agents began complaining on a regular basis about the sale of large quantities of whiskey in the settlements bordering the reservation and demanding that stronger measures be taken to curb this trade.[20] The 1880s and 90s was a turbulent period when gambling, drinking, and carousing inflamed an already difficult situation.

The problem was widespread and serious. For instance, Agent F. T. Bennett stated that the most damaging evil for the Navajo was whiskey. Pointing out that there were traders at numerous locations, from forty to one hundred miles off the reservation, where "whiskey of the vilest description" was sold, he went on to say that this was a direct violation of the law, an incentive for crime, and a factor in impoverishing the Navajos. Also in several councils he held, the chiefs and headmen urged strict control of this traffic, saying, "We have no rivers, streams or lakes of whiskey; why does not the Great Father at Washington, who can do anything he pleases, put a stop to this trade and keep white men from bringing or selling whiskey to us?"[21]

But the problem persisted. One trader who sold liquor encouraged a shooting conflict between cowboys of the Carlisle cattle company and the Navajos, mentioned in the preceding chapter.[22] Newspapers told of incidents such as the one found in the *Durango Herald* of October 31, 1890, in which two women, returning home from Durango, were overtaken by several intoxicated Indians who surrounded the wagon, attempted to take some supplies, and badly frightened them.[23] At the same time, talk of an uprising was whispered about because of friction with the Indians and the fact that "ammunition can be bought everywhere and whiskey or ginger nearly everywhere."[24] Even into the 1900s, there was a trading post on the Little Colorado where "the proprietor sells the Indians whiskey, gambles with them and uses every means possible to defraud and degrade them."[25]

But perhaps one of the most illuminating examples of the extent of use of liquor and gambling on the Navajo Reservation is provided by William T. Shelton, supervisor at the Shiprock Agency in 1903. Speaking of this time, he told of a thirty-five-mile trip he made to Farmington, during which he met "eighteen drunken Indians" coming from Durango. There were also those selling liquor to other Navajos and, to make matters worse, gambling was extensively practiced by almost everyone. He noted that "fifteen or twenty, and sometimes more, would congregate at each of the trading posts during the day and waste their time and money gambling. At some of the posts the traders kept a 'tin horn' gambler at their store for the purpose of getting a crowd together and beating them out of their money."[26]

By the end of the second year (1904–5), Shelton claimed to have put a lid on this activity by gaining the "cooperation of the older and more influential Indians, convincing them that gambling was bad business and detrimental to the best interests of the reservation." For battle trophies from the war against gambling, he collected more than three bushels of playing cards. As for the whiskey traffic, he slowed it by assigning an apprehended first-time offender ten days of work at the agency, a second offender twenty days, with an additional ten days for each additional infraction. In the next ten years there were only eleven drinkers brought in for punishment, leading Shelton to boast, "I doubt if there is a community in the United States more free from whiskey, drinking and gambling than this reservation."[27] While this seems idealistic, Shelton's control was something that had not been possible until the agency was established to help patrol the liquor traffic on the northern boundaries of the reservation.

Control of alcohol sales in the 1880s and 90s had no such force. Liquor was provided from two primary sources. Most vendors were Mexicans operating out of their communities in New Mexico below the Southern Ute Reservation.[28] Part of this contact was brought about by the Navajos going off their lands to sell wool, where they met Mexicans who made their living by gambling and furnishing whiskey.[29] This created a particularly difficult problem when it came time to convict them in a court of law. For example, Agent Plummer reported on June 5, 1894, that whiskey was being sold at certain places in New Mexico but that jury members of Mexican ancestry were slow to find their fellow countrymen guilty. Since an Indian's testimony was not acceptable in court, and since deputy marshals and other law enforcement officers were paid for arresting people, not convicting them, Plummer suggested that a special agent concerned solely with liquor traffic be assigned to the reservation.[30]

But if the Navajo trade was strong, the Southern Ute trade was even stronger. Surrounded by "a mixed population some of which are of the worst element in the country," the Utes lived on the borders of villages where bootleg alcohol was produced.[31] One agent claimed that the Mexicans who lived near the Indians had no "visible means of support, deriving a livelihood from them [Utes] by gambling, bootlegging whiskey, etc." and that a lot of the bothersome "crime and theft can be traced to Mexican origin."[32] Although no definite proof has been found, it seems likely that the trade spread from the Utes, who also served as middlemen to the Navajos on the northern boundary. This assumption is based on the constant interaction between these groups during this period.

A second source of liquor for the Navajo was the border towns in Colorado. While some residents feared the effects of alcohol on the Indians, making them "like wild beasts . . . who would some day cause a massacre," there were those vendors who cared only for profit.[33] Durango and Cortez each had their share of peddlers who were successful in selling but difficult to catch.[34]

The laws enacted to stop this liquor traffic were more specific than those concerned with trading. A peddler faced a $300 fine and two years' imprisonment if found guilty of providing alcohol to Indians either on or off the reservation.[35] Licensed traders were put under special obligation to help curb the sale of liquor since "a drunken Indian is a condensed and intensified savage let loose on the community to commit crimes the blackest in the calendar." If the trader failed to report an offense, his license was revoked and he was removed from the reservation. The ultimate reason for stopping this activity was that the Indians could not be Christianized and civilized as long as "drunkards, gamblers and whiskey traders" could demoralize and debauch them.[36]

An agent actually exercised preventive measures in at least one instance, when a trader was queried about his use of liquor. Correspondence noted that this trader used stimulants only when he considered such treatment necessary and that his character was of a high quality, as was his family's reputation. Nevertheless, the rules were clear: he had no choice but to leave the reservation, since it was difficult to "discriminate between intoxication produced by the use of liquor when considered necessary and produced otherwise."[37] Another would-be trader was identified as using alcohol "very moderately"; he was told to abstain totally in order to receive his license.

Although the laws were both strict and specific, the problem of enforcing them was tremendous. Indian agents, special agents, the military, and civilians all took part at one time or another, but the record of convictions does not reflect the extent of the trade. An example of law enforcement problems is found on the Southern Ute Reservation in 1887. Special Agent M. Armstrong started on the trail of whiskey peddlers who operated along the San Juan. According to railroad workers, Indians were getting liquor from a gang of Mexicans, who left the alcohol in old dugouts beside the railroad tracks. Upon entering some of these huts, Armstrong found evidence, in the form of recently emptied bottles strewn about the floor. Armstrong determined that some of the whiskey was supplied from Durango, some from Pagosa Springs, and some from the Mexican settlements nearby. Further investigation showed that liquor was smuggled in boxes marked hardware, but this plan was foiled by suspicious railroad workers. Often, the selling was done at night, with the goods left unattended at a prearranged location, making it difficult to tie people, places, and sales into a unified court case that resulted in conviction.[38]

On one occasion, the law was too late to protect a bootlegger from his own reward. In April 1888 a white man mounted on a burro came onto the Navajo Reservation from Ute lands. He sold liquor to two Navajos—one twelve, the other twenty-four years of age—and then got into an argument that resulted in his death. His body was thrown into the San Juan. Indians notified the agent, who dispatched eleven Navajo police to bring the two Indians to the agency, but this action was frustrated, his men returning after a confrontation with more than 100 Navajos. This group protected the murderers, who felt they had performed a service by getting rid of the whiskey peddler. White people gave further encouragement by telling the Navajos that they had done a good thing and should not be punished. The guilty parties were never brought to justice.[39]

On a more positive note, one of the better-coordinated efforts of trade along the San Juan and Little Colorado rivers was that of the Mormons. While their record is not unblemished, they recognized early in their frontier experience that trade was both profitable and, if handled properly, a means to maintain friendly relations with Indians. As early as 1854, a group from Springville, Utah, launched a trading expedition south of the San Juan. Desiring to barter with the Navajos for livestock, blankets, and silver jewelry, the Mormons visited the Indians but found them initially hostile. An exaggerated report said the Navajos had just a few days before "killed, boiled and eaten a white man," and though they conducted some trade, the party returned to friendly territory after a short time.[40] But even in this difficult situation, the leader of the group realized that "trade is the best letter of introduction a white man can take among Indians."

Peaceful practices of exchange between the Mormons and the Navajos were based on policies established by Brigham Young and a foundation laid by explorer-traders like Jacob Hamblin and Thales Haskell.[41] As early as 1873, the Navajo agent reported a heavy trade in woven blankets with the Mormons in Utah, while soon after settlements started spreading south along the Little Colorado.[42] But during the period from the 1870s to mid-1880s, one of the most frequently recurring concerns felt by outsiders about Mormon trade was that the Mormons were conspiring to unite the Navajos, Utes, and Paiutes against the U.S. government. No doubt the Mountain Meadows Massacre in 1857 gave an air of credibility to later rumors. Certainly the heavy trade of arms and ammunition at the Elk Mountain Mission in 1855 helped encourage these beliefs, as did a reported meeting of Navajos, Utes, and Paiutes in the Navajo Mountain area in 1859. At this gathering, Mormons gave shirts, beads, and powder to encourage friendly relations among the three tribes for the purpose of furthering Mormon goals of defense. It is difficult to determine exactly how serious this attempt to unify was; in any case, it was ineffective because of growing Ute and Navajo hostility in the 1860s.[43]

That guns were important to both Mormons and Navajos during the 1870s and 80s cannot be doubted. One of the best examples of this is provided by Don Maguire, a freelance trader who made several expeditions into the Southwest, one of which took him to the settlements on the Little Colorado in 1878–79. He had with him a large number of government muskets, carbines, pistols, and ammunition—much of which he sold to Lot Smith, a Mormon leader, and others. The Saints purchased the weapons, for $600, because they believed themselves in constant danger from Navajos and Apaches. Maguire charged three times what he had paid for the weapons. Soon after this, a group of Hopis appeared and purchased 10 rifles, 5 carbines, 5 pistols, and 1,000 rounds of ammunition.[44]

Maguire then traveled to Moenkopi, where he rented the home of licensed Mormon trader Ben Hawley and proceeded to sell the rest of the firearms. Hawley's usual fare consisted of such innocuous items as tobacco, calico, shirts, shoes, trousers, paint, and beads, so one wonders how he justified opening up his store to sell weapons when it was expressly forbidden by government regulation. Maguire stayed there four days, raking in 55 pounds of silver jewelry, 150 blankets, 31 spurs, and 50 other objects of Navajo manufacture, for

40 rifles, 17 pistols, 1,500 rounds of ammunition, and the usual knives, beads, paint, and cloth. After the exchanges were completed, he entertained all those present with two meals of mutton, potatoes, and bread, then waited for his guests to depart before moving north. His bartered items were eventually sold in New York City for a good profit.[45]

While this was not Mormon trading in its purest sense, this episode certainly occurred with the approval of local Mormons. Perhaps it also helped keep alive the fear that Mormons were supplying weapons to the Indians. Again in 1881, reports started to filter into Washington of a Mormon conspiracy in which Navajos, Utes, and Paiutes living in Arizona, New Mexico, and Utah were "freely furnished with arms and provisions by Mormons who are affiliating with the Indians and giving them all the whiskey they want." Tentatively, an outbreak was expected in the spring.[46]

Navajo Agent Galen Eastman investigated and reported that one of his most reliable headmen from the northwestern part of the reservation felt that all was quiet, that no arms or whiskey were being sold, and that there was no discontent. Eastman then turned the tables on Thomas F. Hopkins, author of the letter that prompted the investigation, saying that he was fomenting trouble to get what he wanted. The agent suggested that he could visit Hopkins and his associates and thus find the real trouble. While Eastman agreed that an illegal trade did exist along the Atlantic and Pacific Railroad and in St. Johns, Arizona, he exonerated the Mormons by stating, "While I am not an admirer of Mormonism, yet so far as my observation goes, they are peacefully inclined and are friendly with all Indians and treat them kindly and for these reasons their stock is safe and their leaders assure me they never permit their people to sell whiskey and arms to them, and I believe they do not to any considerable extent."[47] Hopkins, a person described as controlling eastern capital in mining businesses in Maricopa County, Arizona, created no further trouble. His apparent ploy to harass the Mormons and expand his operations failed.

Another problem occurred when gentile traders attempted to take over in the absence of Mormon traders. C. L. Christensen, a settler in the Moenkopi area, told how he returned home in 1885 from an extended trip and found the old fort taken over by gentiles who had converted it into a trade center backed by the Spiegelberg Brothers of Albuquerque. Representing these wool buyers, the traders united in an attempt to incite Hopis and Navajos against the Mormons and threatened to hang Christensen if he did not stop influencing the Indians. This influence included counseling them "to quit lying, stealing, card playing, riding Mormon, American or Indian horses that did not belong to them, and last and worst of all, adultery . . . as a number of these refined gentlemen depend upon the young girls and women for gratification of the lusts of the flesh."[48] From an economic standpoint, these traders were interested in reaping the same type of profit that Christensen reported a couple of weeks later when he went to Winslow, Arizona, and loaded 1,762 pounds of wool at a dollar a pound onto the Atlantic and Pacific Railroad for the Sam Dutlinhuffer and Company Wool Merchants of Moenkopi.[49] Money was made by both factions involved in the trading business.

At the same time the Mormons were developing trade along the Little Colorado, another group was building its posts in the new community of Bluff, Utah. Founded in 1880, this town soon became involved in trade with Navajos and Utes on both an individual and group basis. Also, shortly after the main body of Mormons went through the Hole-in-the-Rock, they were joined by William Hyde, a Mormon merchant from Salt Lake City who opened a trading post in Montezuma Creek eighteen miles above Bluff.

While Hyde's business flourished—growing into at least two other posts in the Four Corners area—his experience serves as an interesting illustration of the diversity of the life of a trader. For instance, his sixteen-year-old daughter, Parfenia, established the first district school in the fall of 1880.[50] She was also involved in a one-sided love affair when a young Ute warrior named Sanop's Boy threatened William Hyde with death if he did not turn over his daughter for marriage. Apparently the Indian was pacified, since no war broke out, and Parfenia soon married Amasa Barton, another Mormon trader and business partner to Hyde.[51]

By February 1881, Montezuma Creek had seven families with room for four times that number. Survival depended as much on home industry and farming as on trading, so Hyde built an irrigation wheel sixteen feet in diameter with a twelve-foot reach that lifted 23,000 gallons of water an hour into the ditches.[52] The wheel remained in operation for three years before being washed down the San Juan on June 8, 1884, in a flood that took much of the Aneth and Montezuma Creek communities with it. The disaster closed out Hyde's operation on this part of the river, but with his post at Peak City, Colorado, and another further down the San Juan, the Hyde and Barton Trading Company continued to prosper.[53]

It is also interesting to note that Hyde, like the Mormons on the Little Colorado, was not free from accusations of conspiracy. In 1884, two miners by the name of Samuel T. Walcott and James McNally were killed while traveling near Navajo Mountain. Hyde's trading post below Bluff operated a ferry, so news of the surrounding area funneled in to this point. He received word of the murder ten days before the incident became public knowledge, as his daughter told another trader. Henry L. Mitchell also got word of this news and wrote to a friend of Walcott, an armchair investigator named Fred Fickey, living in Baltimore, Maryland. Fickey concluded with Mitchell's help that Walcott had been more afraid of the Mormons than the Indians, that Hyde was the "prime actor or originator of the affair," and that the Indians would confirm this fact.[54] A subsequent investigation by the agent, Navajo police, and the military exonerated Hyde, placing the blame on four Navajos who visited Walcott's camp to trade.

Yet violence also struck Mormon trading posts. Amasa Barton ran a store and ferry at Rincon, a natural crossing place eight miles below Bluff. Described as a "tidy, orderly, thrifty, resourceful, honest and all around good citizen," Barton was a Mormon in good standing when in 1885 he requested permission to establish this post away from the confines of Bluff City proper.[55] Bishop Jens Nielson was not anxious to grant this favor, which was contrary to advice given by church authorities, so he left the final decision to Barton, who located his store in a place that served both Indians and local stockmen.[56]

On June 9, 1887, two Indians visited the post, one of whom had earlier pawned a string of beads, which he now wanted back for two dollars less. An argument ensued, and as the trader stooped to go under the counter, the Indians slipped a rope around his neck and pinioned his arms, so that he fell to the floor. One Indian drew his pistol and shot Barton in the head, then accidentally placed a round in his partner's chest. Another shot was fired into Barton's skull, while the wounded Navajo ran outside the store and died. William Hyde's wife and daughter were present, but Barton warned them to stay away until the Indians departed, the survivor carrying his dead friend to the ferry and then crossing the river. Soon the survivor returned with other Navajos; they demanded the key to the store, from which they removed $400 worth of goods. Barton died on June 16, just a few days after sixty Navajos visited Bluff to confront the fifteen Mormon families living there. A threat by the settlers to introduce soldiers into the conflict induced the Indians to restore amicable relations.[57] This incident was the exception and not the rule in Mormon-Navajo trade relations.

Perhaps the most successful Mormon group bartering venture on the northern boundary of the reservation was that of the San Juan or Bluff Co-op. Organized on April 29, 1882, this enterprise stayed in operation until January 21, 1920, at which time it was sold to an individual. The first board was composed of influential men in the Mormon hierarchy of Bluff: Platte D. Lyman, president; Bishop Jens Nielson, vice president; Charles E. Walton, Kumen Jones, and Hyrum Perkins, directors; and Joseph H. Lyman, salesman.[58] In five months this venture had paid a 10 percent dividend, which in one year increased to 25 percent.[59]

At first a small amount of freight was hauled from Escalante over the Hole-in-the-Rock Trail to Bluff and its trading posts.[60] But it did not take long to form business connections with southwestern Colorado, as the co-op moved merchandise by way of Navajo Springs, Mancos, Durango, and Alamosa. Shipping time took only ten days round-trip and provided necessary employment for the men of Bluff in between their farm responsibilities. Many of these freighters were also stockholders in the company. The trade with Colorado provided a side benefit evident on wash days when the children's underwear, which was made out of flour sacks stamped "Pride of Durango," was hung out to dry.[61]

As for the actual trading at the Co-op, the business transactions were similar to those of most posts. The owners hired a young man to operate a ferry on the river. They purchased blankets, pelts, silver, and wool, the latter often being washed, carded, spun, and dyed with roots and bark, then knitted into stockings or woven into cloth. One visitor described the interior of the store as having an "L-shaped counter [which] allowed them [Indians] a space about eight by twelve feet, and in this narrow area they jostled each other, smoking and laughing and giggling with the clerk in their high keyed lingo for higher prices on their wares."[62]

There was also a log warehouse in which raw wool was stored. An amusing story concerning this building involved a Ute named Mike Moenkopi, who came occasionally to trade for necessities. The wool he brought for payment was often the same amount found missing in the warehouse, having been removed from an unchinked crack between the logs. Versions of the tale differ as to how Mike was caught, but one account tells of a carefully laid wolf trap that clamped hold of his hand on the far side of the wall. The captors released the Indian after a little physical punishment.[63]

By the late 1890s and early 1900s, trading posts along the San Juan were meeting the needs of the Navajos, who were increasingly dependent on the economic system of the white man. The heyday of the trader was yet to come, but the perceived need for manufactured goods existed. An example of this growing dependence was provided by a Navajo named Left Handed when he first entered a trading post in the 1880s:

> When we got there the door was open and that was the store. Lots of things were in that house. On the shelves lay bundles of red flannel and white cloth and dishes, and from the ceiling hung buckets of different sizes and scarfs of all colors. Everything was new to me. I stood and looked thinking, "What wonderful things they are." Old Man Thankful started trading. He bought a roll of black leather, a bundle of white cloth and a bundle of red flannel. . . . He also bought a bucket and bracelet which my mother had asked for and a scarf and a black hat for my father.[64]

The trading posts were heavily dependent upon wool blankets and furs. Over-hunting of deer became a serious problem, especially as the reservation became more clearly defined, the Utes and Navajos more closely watched, and the game wardens stricter in enforcing hunting laws. Large numbers of deer were killed for the hide trade, while infuriated citizens sent letters and petitions to state governors, Indian agents, and the Commissioner of Indian Affairs, demanding a halt to the slaughter. By 1890 this phenomenon was occurring throughout the western states to such an extent that the Bureau of Indian Affairs sent a letter to the agents, directing them to counsel their tribal members as to the game laws. In short, the regulation said that the right to hunt off the reservation was recognized but gave only the privilege of killing "game as may be necessary to supply the needs of the Indians and that the slaughter of wild animals in vast numbers for hides only . . . is as much a violation of the treaty as an absolute prohibition on the part of the United States against the exercise of such privilege would be. . . . In view of the settlement of the country and consequent disappearance of the game, the time has long since gone by when the Indians can live by the chase."[65] And yet the price of hides offered a practical way to get money. In 1878, for instance, the Indians sold buckskins in large volume to traders who shipped them to the railroad at a rate of $1,000 a ton.[66] In 1890, trading posts on the San Juan offered fifty cents a hide with the Navajos taking advantage of the opportunity.[67]

Another way to earn money was through the sale of wool and blankets. A common practice used to avoid freighting problems in a roadless wilderness was the sheep drive in which Navajos herded their livestock to an area opposite the post and there sheared them. A boat then crossed the river and picked up the large seven-to-nine-foot-long sacks of wool, which the Navajos accompanied to the post. There, the trader paid the Indians—the amount was between fifteen and seventeen dollars a sack in 1890—and encouraged them to spend most of their money in the store, thus keeping the cash close to home for the trader. They then stored some of the wool for sale in the cold winter months when the Navajos needed it for weaving; blankets were sold to the trader for between four and seven dollars.[68] This trade in woven goods continued to expand so that by 1914 it provided a $700,000 income for the reservation.[69]

One of the most important principles involved in trading during this and subsequent periods was that of pawn. Ideally, an Indian could bring anything of value—blankets, silver, guns, and so forth—and leave it at a post to be redeemed later for cash. While this practice could benefit both parties, much depended on the character of the trader and the flow of the economy. The government tried to ensure that "only a proper person engaged in such trade."[70] A number of posts encouraged competition to keep costs low on the reservation, since it was forbidden to form a monopoly to establish uniform prices to the disadvantage of the Navajos.[71] As late as 1905, a government report insisted that the "best source of competition is the approach of white towns to the reservation boundary and the opening of reservation tracts to white occupancy. . . . Nevertheless, since the licensed trader is nearest the Indians, he continues to have some advantage over an outsider in making sales and collecting debts and his personal influence and example still go a good way with our red brother."[72]

Traders also encouraged some of the Indians to move toward a wage economy. During the 1890s and early 1900s one Navajo, Old Mexican, had many such opportunities as he lived and worked around the Aneth-Shiprock area. One of his primary sources of income was freighting, usually to either Cortez or Mancos. For a three-day round trip to Cortez, the trader paid him ten dollars, and for a trip to Mancos, twelve.[73] Posts also hired Navajos to act as guides across the reservation, to attend exhibition dances in Durango and other cities, to promote the Shiprock Agency Fairs started in 1909, to construct roads and irrigation ditches, and to help find and excavate Anasazi ruins in the Four Corners area. The most famous traders to hire Navajos for excavations were John and Richard Wetherill.[74]

It is difficult to estimate how many Navajos were attracted to a single post along the San Juan during the period 1870 to 1910, since so much depended on economic, political, and social events. Perhaps the best indication comes from a report by Colonel George W. Hunter, who traveled through the northern part of the reservation in 1908 to study the conditions and temperament of the Navajo shortly after the explosive Bai-alil-le affair.[75] Hunter held a large council at the Wetherill post in Oljato; from this meeting and the information garnered from the traders, he determined that a total of 1,512 Navajos, Utes, and Paiutes lived in approximately a sixty-mile radius.[76] How many of these frequented the Oljato post on a regular basis was not known, but one of Hunter's officers visited Bluff at the same time and reported that 950 adult Navajos had traded there during the year and that about half of these had homes within a sixy-mile radius.[77]

By 1910 certain changes either had occurred or were starting to occur that caused a shift in the old trading practices. Although some of the changes were gradual and imperceptible, others were easily identified. For example, the government built the first of a series of bridges across the San Juan, Colorado, and Little Colorado rivers, eliminating the need for ferries while opening up the northern part of the reservation to increased vehicular traffic. The first bridge was under construction in 1909 near the Shiprock Agency School, followed by bridges at Mexican Hat (1909), Tanner's Crossing (1910), and Lee's Ferry (1925).[78]

There existed now more trading posts on the reservation than ever before. A report issued in 1936 stated that of the forty-nine posts visited on Navajo lands, eleven had been established before 1900 and thirty-eight had been introduced since that time. An additional thirty were not visited and so could not provide data.[79] There was also a tightening of control and more interest expressed in development by the Bureau of Indian Affairs through agents like William T. Shelton, working out of Shiprock. Agency police, trade fairs, agricultural projects, Christian missions, and boarding schools all helped to change the strength and quality of the old-time magnetism that drew Navajos to the borders to trade.

Thus by 1910, law, order, education, and control were established at an unprecedented rate, making impractical and undesirable the more free wheeling days of the 1870s and 80s. This is not to suggest that all was calm, but only that the old ways were fading. This set the stage for a new era—the heyday of the trading post—starting in the early 1900s.

The experience of the early trading posts on the northern Navajo frontier was dynamic. The ebb and flow of the institution rose and fell with the general American economy as well as local events. Mormons and gentiles both operated stores successfully, creating an atmosphere of competition for business.

The Navajos, on the other hand, were introduced to desirable goods from the general economy, which encouraged a greater dependence on these products. Liquor sales, gambling, and sales of arms and ammunition created special problems that did not subside until the establishment of a local governing agency at Shiprock in 1903 and the careful demarcation of reservation boundaries, the topic of the next chapter.

7 / Boundaries, Bonanzas, and Bickering: Consolidation of the Northern Navajo Frontier, 1870–1905

Nati'nesthani, He Who Teaches Himself, floated down the San Juan River in a cottonwood log hollowed out for him by the gods. His journey was prompted by problems at home and a search for new opportunities; his only companion was a pet turkey, ceremonially prepared to help the young man. Adventure followed adventure, but finally Nati'nesthani reached the end of the river where he left his log and sat pondering his future. Speaking to his companion he said, "My pet, what a beautiful farm I could make here if I only had the seeds." The bird responded by spreading its wings, walking in the four cardinal directions and at each point dropping seeds of corn, pumpkin, beans, and melons. These were soon planted and eventually harvested by the hero, who at the end of the story returns to his farm on the river, having found a wife, survived supernatural tests, and achieved peace with a dangerous foe. He lives there still.[1]

This myth, recorded by Washington Matthews in 1897, explains some of the beliefs behind the "Plume Way" and other ceremonies. But more important, it recognizes the San Juan River as a fruitful area for the Navajo to practice agriculture. From 1870 to 1905, the people of this region became embroiled in a series of disputes over land that involved Navajos and Utes against white settlers and miners, as each group tried to establish and then maintain control of the land. This was also a period when the Navajos, like He Who Teaches Himself, began to adopt new agricultural techniques under the direction of the federal government, while still trying to maintain their traditional values. The problems encountered in Navajo interaction with Mormons, gentile settlers, cattle companies, trading posts, and others had a cumulative effect that reached fruition in this period. By 1900, government policies defined the boundaries of the northern part of the reservation in such a way that Navajo expansion onto the public domain was accented with reservation lands being added and protected. But this came about only after a turbulent period of give and take, which is the topic of this chapter.

In the 1870s and 80s, the Four Corners area saw a marked increase in white population. Mormon and gentile settlers, cattle companies, mining interests, the railroad, and the subsequent establishment of towns all served to change the Indians' lifestyle. Perhaps the most permanent force of change was the settler, whose homesteading of the public domain centered on the most important of natural resources—water. The Navajos also sought water. As early as 1872, Navajo agents looked to the San Juan as the most practical place to encourage their charges to become more dependent on agriculture. Although the Navajos had always been involved in farming on a limited scale—on flood plains and perennial streams, using small-scale irrigation or dry farming—the agents were now hoping for large acres of planted crops, dependent on more complex irrigation systems. High yields in agriculture were a goal stated in the *Report of the Commissioner of Indian Affairs* throughout this period.

There were two reasons for this. First, by increasing the amount and variety of food grown by the Indians, the government could theoretically decrease expenses involved in purchasing and shipping supplies. In reality, the Navajos and Utes during this period depended upon the government for survival, though in many instances they made valiant attempts to become more self-sufficient. Second, many experts viewed agriculture as a tool that would move the Indian from "blanket" to overalls and from barbarism to civilization. Whether or not farming was practical in all geographic regions, government representatives saw it as a tool to promote change. Although the reservation at this time comprised 3,328,000 acres in northwestern New Mexico and northeastern Arizona, there were few places in this desert land that could support intensive agriculture for the estimated 9,114 Navajos living there.[2]

So it was that in 1872 the government launched a formal attempt to identify a site that could be developed as a garden spot for the ever-increasing number of Navajos. Agent James H. Miller and B. M. Thomas, agency farmer, realized that the agricultural returns of the past year at their headquarters in Fort Defiance were meager at best. In June, therefore, the two men along with a trader and interpreter set out for the San Juan Valley to find a place to establish at least a subagency to be used eventually as the main post. Unfortunately, as this party camped along the river two Utes attacked them and in the act of stealing the horses killed Miller.[3] This incident highlights one reason why this northern part of the reservation was not already heavily populated. Anxiety over the Utes kept most Navajos in check. They remembered the "Fearing Time" of the late 1850s and 60s, when Kit Carson encouraged Utes to prey on their enemies. Some groups of Navajos befriended the Utes and Paiutes in the area, but far larger numbers considered the Utes dangerous.

Yet Miller's death and the Navajo's fear were still not enough to discourage the Superintendent of Indian Affairs, Nathaniel Pope, who wrote that "should the farming facilities in the San Juan Valley prove to be as reported, that the Department will be almost entirely relieved of the expense of furnishing subsistence. Aside from this, the possession of large herds of stock . . . will tend to keep them at home and peaceable."[4] In reality, events proved the opposite.

The next few years witnessed fluctuations of interest in the project. Cost estimates ranged from $15,000 to $57,500, with the scope of the undertaking varying from a temporary summer camp to be used only for agricultural purposes to a full-time agency with school, chapel, irrigation ditches, and a new road system to tie in with the Denver and Rio Grande Railroad, which by this time was completed to Fort Garland, Colorado.[5] Additional factors helped encourage change, such as a land grant to the Atlantic and Pacific Railroad on the southern end of the reservation, blocking a desired extension, which in turn fostered the idea of settling Navajos to the north.[6] The belief was that if the agent located a place on the San Juan, it could provide "all the corn, wheat and vegetables for twice the number of Indians in the tribe."[7] Another belief was that the government should "afford to be a little magnanimous and give to a peaceable and industrious tribe of Indians a few more square miles of barren sand."[8] Thus, by 1880 the way was paved for the northward expansion of the Navajo Reservation, to accompany previous extensions of lands on the west in 1878 and the east in 1880.[9]

The Southern Utes, however, were in a similar situation: Their agency had been moved from Abiquiu to Ignacio in southern Colorado. Although the new reservation had more streams—La Plata, Animas, Florida, Los Pinos, and Piedra—the San Juan tied all of them together as a primary source of water. The Ute agent, George Manypenny, traveled over much of the reservation trying to determine what lands were most suitable for agriculture. Many of the river valleys were appropriate for cultivation, but Manypenny received increasing pressure from white settlers who had similar ideas. He would not accede to their desire to have the Utes settled on barren wasteland, but at the same time he realized that "to assume that the Utes will not be disturbed but permitted to dwell in peace, would be to nurture a delusion of the gravest kind."[10] Thus, as the Utes were being squeezed into the southwestern corner of Colorado, the Navajos were being encouraged to move into the northern reaches of their reservation in the Four Corners area.

The natural result was conflict, which characterized life in this region during the 1880s and first half of the 1890s, though sporadic trouble persisted into the early 1900s. Incidents ranged from murder to destruction of property and intimidation; the catalog of crimes is extensive. Examples of Navajo and Ute activities, however, illustrate the problems faced by the settlers. The most common offense was begging, stealing, or destroying property. Stolen livestock, ruined fences, demands of food, and threats of harm became so common that many settlers feared leaving their farm and family for only a day. But even when the men were home, incidents occurred. At one ranch in McElmo, Colorado, a man had his tools, harness, and blankets stolen and was then approached by seven Utes who called him "vile names," pulled his ears, told him to "go right now," and then tried to drag him out of his house. He escaped; shots were fired at him, which he returned; and then the Utes pursued him in a cat-and-mouse chase to his neighbor's home where he hid, undetected.[11]

One comparatively minor incident involved George Washington (Ute), a "hideous old cuss," who considered himself a "big Ike." He went to the home of E. T. Walker, a settler whose wife was lying sick in bed. Finding the door and front windows locked, George walked around to her bedroom and "stuck his head in with one of his cursed grunts and so frightened her that she has been confined to her bed with doctor bills for me [Walker] to foot up in consequence of Mr. Washington's call."[12]

The Navajos also did their share of intimidating settlers; constant patrolling by cavalry from Fort Lewis and Fort Wingate, the two military posts used by Navajo agents, helped control the situation.[13] There were also fears that the Navajos and Utes were supporting each other in their attempts to frustrate white settlers, reports to this effect being issued in 1879, 1885, and 1889.[14] Turbulence was characteristic of events in this period and was a part of the Navajos' aggressive defensive activities on the northern Navajo frontier.

One of the pressing questions asked by the white settler was how the Navajos could justify being away from the reservation. Part of the problem stemmed from the Navajo lifestyle. Ever-increasing herds of sheep and a growing population placed greater demands on the lands for both agricultural and grazing purposes. Estimates of the number of Navajos off the reservation were as high as 8,000; although this figure seems excessive, it emphasizes that many Indians chose to look for greener pastures.[15] The natural place to find free land was the public domain, since the Navajos had as much right to use it for grazing and homesteading purposes as did their white neighbors. This was the ideal; the reality proved quite different. In 1885, Navajo Agent John H. Bowman addressed this problem in his annual report:

> The non-confinement of these Indians to their reservation will soon be the important issue of this section and one with which your office must deal. The country around here is fast being settled up with whites; earnest men, most of whom do not believe that an Indian has any business off of his reservation; men who have no great love for them anyway and who will be inclined to make them stand aside if they get in their way. It is impossible for these Indians to understand our land laws or the system of public surveys and harder still for

> them to comply with the requirements of the homestead laws.[16]

Another difficulty the Indians faced was the unscrupulous machinations of white men, who took unfair advantage of the Navajos' lack of familiarity with the law. For example, one Indian lived for twelve years on a piece of property located 100 miles from the reservation. On it he raised his family of seven children, built a house and corral, and was generally productive. But when he went to Santa Fe to file for a land title, he gave his $160 fee to a man who pretended to be the land agent and who then absconded with the money. The Navajo notified the authorities but nothing was done.[17]

Still others opposed giving more land to the Navajos, believing that the Indians already had enough. There had been recent additions made to the reservation and to add more would compound the folly. Major General John Pope, Commander of the Department of the Missouri, reasoned, "If these Indians want more land, because of their great prosperity, surely they can afford to buy it as well as the whites. . . . That the white settlers will make far better use of the land than the Indians is certain."[18]

Other people closer to the problem felt differently. Special Agent William Parsons noted that in some places Navajos and whites were trying to cultivate the same quarter section of land and that "the only permanent solution of the difficulty on the San Juan River will be to add all the land south of that river to the Navajo Reservation. . . . It is in fact all desert and mountain with the exception of 2,000 acres of bottom land susceptible of irrigation. . . . This land the Navajo must have in order to get to water with their herds and flocks."[19]

On May 17, 1884, President Chester A. Arthur signed an executive order expanding the northern part of the reservation into Utah to the south side of the San Juan River, hoping to eliminate conflict over lands by providing official recognition of Navajo rights. In the same order, however, a small portion of land in New Mexico, which had been made part of the reservation by an executive order on January 6, 1880, was now removed from Navajo control.

Twenty-one Anglo families utilizing this land in the corner of northwestern New Mexico favored the policy of restoring to the public domain a portion of Township 29 north, Ranges 14, 15, and 16 west, located south of the river.[20] The Indians, however, were adamantly opposed to giving up this territory, since to do so prevented access to the water they needed for their herds, and this in turn made the land fifty to seventy miles back from the river unusable for grazing purposes. A conflict ensued that legally ended on April 24, 1886, by an executive order restoring the land to the Navajos. The settlers were slow to respond, both sides demanding their rights, while the Navajos obtained "an ample supply of the best ammunition" in order to "maintain these possessions and their just rights as they understand them."[21] This is a good example of the Navajos' defensive policy in operation.

Subsequently, two cavalry troops were stationed on the river to help prevent trouble and to enforce evacuation of the white settlers, twelve to fifteen of whom "manifested a dogged determination to stay until paid for their improvements."[22] Further investigation of the various claims coming from this area revealed that only three of the settlers had actually made improvements like log cabins or farms, that in three places access to the river was denied by hostile claimants who threatened violence, and that the Indians had just as bitter feelings towards the settlers but had shown forbearance in avoiding trouble.[23] The government removed the settlers by November 1887, withdrew the cavalry, and gave the job of seeing that the homesteaders did not return to one lieutenant and five privates of the Indian police force.[24] The Navajos also helped ensure that the settlers would stay out of the area by destroying any "improvements" on the land. Claims of twenty-one whites were settled by June 1889, the amounts ranging from $14.66 to $1,237.71 with an aggregate sum of $10,000.[25] Fortunately, no bloodshed occurred during this transfer of property.

But the extension of reservation lands proved to be of only temporary value in stopping Navajo expansion. The agent's estimates of the numbers of off-reservation Navajos continued to climb, reaching 10,000 for the entire reservation in 1889.[26] He received letters and petitions from residents and officials in Utah, Colorado, Arizona, and New Mexico, complaining of Navajo activities ranging from flooding an area with large sheep herds to small parties of livestock thieves roaming the territory. These provide further examples of Navajos aggressively using the surrounding borderlands.

Even the Ute agent, Charles Bartholomew, who was struggling to introduce agriculture on this reservation, complained of Navajo encroachment. Writing to the Navajo agent, he charged that "the western part of this reserve was over run with your Navajo Indians. . . . Our Utes are very anxious that you keep your Indians at home. They are afraid that the Navajos will commit some overt act which will cause the whites to retaliate and mistaking the acts of the Navajos for the Utes. This could not very well occur if you will keep your Indians across the line and I am anxious that this should be done."[27] The Navajo agent's response was conciliatory. He pointed out that with a population of 25,000 spread over a territory of about 11,000 square miles, it was hard to watch everyone, but that if he could "catch and punish a few troublesome members of the tribe," the news would spread over the reservation to produce the desired effect.[28] He also dispatched Navajo police to drive the offenders back to the appropriate reservation, with instructions that no one was to leave again without a pass from the agent.

This solution, however, was only temporary. As late as 1901, Ute Agent Joseph O. Smith wrote to the Commissioner of Indian Affairs, stating there were eight or ten Navajo families on his reservation who claimed to have been there for five or six years but who should be removed. The Navajo agent responded that he was unaware of this situation and that the Navajos should be brought back after they harvested their crops, to which the Commissioner agreed.[29]

Once the government established the boundaries of the northern part of the reservation, interest grew in implementing agricultural plans. It was a formidable undertaking to cultivate these lands, which were described by one agent as "my ideal of a desert; and although very large, it might have been much larger without covering any land of the least value. It is merely a space on the map of so many degrees and parallels. Three fourths of it is about as valuable for stock grazing as that many acres of clear sky. . . . The valleys are composed of sand formed by wash and erosion; no soil worthy of the name."[30] Other estimates, not as pessimistic, looked to the San Juan with the hope that, if the Navajos dug a large irrigation ditch, from 5,000 to 7,000 acres "could be made into a complete garden."[31]

Keeping this goal in mind, the government ordered a general survey of the reservation in 1892 "with a view to establishing and maintaining a system of irrigation and developing a stock water supply sufficient for the Navajo Indians. . . . That an estimate of the cost of constructing the proposed ditches, dams . . . be submitted in detail," and that a complete report be made concerning feasibility.[32] The study, finished in 1893, contained a section on the San Juan that mentioned the dry washes on the northern side of the river and recommended that the settlers of Bluff, Utah, be given a contract to develop a three-mile-long ditch at a cost of $650 to irrigate an estimated 260 acres of land.[33] No mention was made, however, of lands further east along the San Juan in New Mexico.

The 1890s were characterized by severe drought, early frosts, and miserable harvests, thus underscoring the need to develop a steady flow of water. The citizens of Farmington, New Mexico, observed the struggles of the Navajos as crops failed and livestock ranged farther from their appointed lands to graze. Surprisingly, the settlers wrote to the Secretary of the Interior requesting help and defending the character of their neighbors. They insisted that the Navajos were not professional beggars but were in need of immediate governmental assistance, since their situation had grown so bad that they were now eating their horses. Many Indians were expected to die in the spring of 1895, if something was not done.[34] The people of Bluff wrote a similar letter in 1902, saying that the past nine years had left the Navajos without any means of subsistence.[35] One Indian on the lower San Juan was so anxious to change his situation that he rode 100 miles in the winter to ask the agent to help reconstruct a ditch that had fallen in disrepair.[36]

The agents were not insensitive to the Navajos' plight. One man bought 10,000 pounds of flour on his own initiative, hoping that the government would reimburse him when it realized how serious the situation was.[37] Pleas for additional irrigation development funds were made through government channels while further studies were conducted to ensure effective expenditures.

But one of the most interesting forms of aid came to the northern Navajo in the guise of the Methodist Ladies Home Missionary Society of New York, who in 1891 built a parsonage and church in Jewett, New Mexico.[38] Initially assigned to teach school, Field Matron Mary Eldridge quickly became involved in the fundamental needs of health and welfare. Logging in long hours of Indian instruction in 1893—305 in cleanliness, 251 in sewing, 347 in sick care, 503 in receiving medicine—and recording a total of 4,680 Navajo visitors in her home, she appears to have been well accepted.[39]

Eldridge's operating expenses ranged between $1,000 and $2,000 per year, which included plows, shovels, axes, hoes, and other implements that citizens loaned to help meet the Indians' agricultural needs. Supporters in the East as well as the Indian Department sent seeds. On one occasion, Eldridge nursed back to health a woman who had been given up to die by the medicine men. According to the agent, "some of the most desperate characters of the tribe who have come under her influence have developed into steady, hard working men."[40] In 1895, Eldridge was able to report that because of the help she received from the Cambridge, Massachusetts, branch of the Indian Relief Association, Navajos who had previously had only one ax and a broken-handled shovel to construct a ditch were provided with sufficient tools to build the "Cambridge Ditch" to serve nearly 600 acres of land.[41] All of this was done in the belief that "irrigation, allotment of land and education of all the children will civilize these people, and the love of God will save them."[42]

Initially the agents were not in favor of missionaries on the reservation. One was reported to have said, "Put those women just as far from the agency as you can; we don't want missionary women watching us and reporting."[43] But subsequent results and reports indicate both admiration of and dependence upon the work done on the San Juan. Agent Constant Williams said of Eldridge that she could "not be too highly commended. Her life is one of hardship and devotion and whatever she undertakes she does well."[44] One visitor from the East felt that "these motherly, warm hearted and courageous women should be upheld by the Government in every way, and every facility should be provided by it to further their legitimate work."[45] Positive reports of this and other missionary activities continued into the early 1900s, until the establishment of the San Juan Agency eclipsed their efforts.

In addition to agriculture and missionary work, another issue confronted the northern Navajos in the 1890s: mining. Interest in the mineral wealth of the San Juan country goes back to the 1850s and 60s as miners moved on Ute territory in southwestern Colorado in a series of strikes. But there was only sporadic interest in Navajo lands, much of which centered on the legendary silver mine alleged to have been discovered at Navajo Mountain by the Navajos in the 1860s.[46] Adding to this tale of secret Navajo mineral wealth were the murders by Paiutes of James Merrick and Ernest Mitchell in 1879, and the deaths of Samuel Walcott and James McNally in 1884.[47]

These incidents, along with others, were the result of anti-white sentiment and greed, rather than any Navajo aversion toward miners, though the

Indians realized the danger of encroachment that miners represented. Proof of this lies in the testimony provided by Navajos through Indian police involved in each instance as well as the fact that Hashkeneinii, around the same time that Walcott and McNally were killed, spent several weeks showing some prospectors the northwestern part of the reservation.[48] Though the miners discovered no precious minerals, this action shows the Navajos did not resent individual miners. In fact, in 1885 one of these men, William F. Williams, and his sons set up a trading post near Navajo Mountain and had the Indians bring in ore samples. These were carelessly put in a sack and later analyzed. One stone had a significant amount of gold in it, but at this late date it was impossible to determine who brought it in or where it came from.[49]

Starting in 1889, however, large groups of miners placed increasing pressure on the northern part of the reservation, and the Indians reacted. Navajo Agent C. E. Vandever prevented a band of prospectors and cowboys that was forming in Gallup from entering Navajo lands. Fired by the report of rich silver and gold lodes, fifty men were preparing to invade the Carrizo Mountains. They were stopped by both the agent and military authorities—or so it was believed.[50]

But by the end of March 1890, eighteen of this group were in the Carrizos holding out against the Indians. The Navajos, under Black Horse, offered half the prospectors' horses to the Utes if they would help rid the area of miners.[51] Two troops of cavalry and the agent evicted the prospectors, warned them not to return, and escorted them off the reservation. Some, however, persisted and came back in June. Vandever feared that "threats of invasion by other parties have been made and other attempts will surely follow, until such time as the Department investigates the extent of the alleged mineral wealth of that region and determines either to close it against miners or open it for development."[52]

This was a prophetic statement. While Vandever was reporting his action concerning the prospectors, local newspapers helped generate increasing interest in the Carrizos. The *Albuquerque Citizen* claimed that "the whole truth has not been told and he [Vandever] believes the district to be much richer in the abundance of precious metals which it contains than the most extravagant accounts have ever represented it to be."[53] The newspaper went on to say that Vandever believed the area should be opened up to miners since Indians cared nothing about mineral wealth, that it was impossible to stop "enterprising white men," that the Carrizo country was "one of the richest gold districts ever yet discovered in the United States," and that the mountains were too rich to remain in the possession of "savages." The *Durango Herald* chimed in, confirming the existence of tremendous wealth and stating, "The whole United States Army could not protect these mountains now that it is known to a certainty that gold exists. It will be the Black Hills over again."[54]

On May 10, 1892, the Navajo Commission met at Fort Wingate and proceeded to the Carrizos to inspect the gold and silver deposits. General A.

McCook, chairman of this committee, was to determine if there was a basis for opening land negotiations with the Indians. After scouring the countryside, geologists, scientists, and prospectors all agreed that the sandstone formations that composed most of the mountain range were barren of precious metals and that the Indians could keep their land.[55]

The Navajo perspective on these events is instructive. Old Mexican, a young man at this time, told how he was called to a meeting at Red Rock by a very old man with white hair and an eagle on his shoulder. This soldier sent out two men each day to prospect for minerals, but they always returned having found nothing. The leader then called the Navajos together and explained that the army had come to help and protect the Indians:

> But the fellows who sent the note to Washington are not going to give up the mountain. Therefore I want you Indians to build houses all around the mountain where there are springs and plenty of water. Those houses will represent a fence around the mountain. . . . The white men who gamble and drink and get into debt, with no way to pay their debts, they are the ones who come to this reservation looking for gold, scheming for some way to pay their debts. Don't let them get a chance to get the best of you. . . . If you ever see another white fellow around here prospecting for gold, saying that he was sent from Washington, don't believe him. If they ever want any more prospecting done, you will see me back again with my men.[56]

Yet the gold fever persisted and only shifted to the lower San Juan where an invasion of miners in 1892 and 1893 caused as much concern to the Mormons in Bluff as it did to the Navajos on the south side of the river. Starting in early November, reports of gold became so numerous that the government revised the executive order of May 17, 1884, in the order of November 19, 1892, restoring to the public domain the lands that lay west of longitude 110° west within the territory of Utah.[57]

Miners reported that this strip of land contained an immense deposit of gold in black sand, which varied from three to six miles in width and about fifteen miles in length, with sand from eighteen to twenty feet in depth.[58] The Atlantic and Pacific Railroad contemplated constructing a feeder line to this gold-rich area. The general consensus was that the Indians had no use for the minerals, so the land should be opened to exploration and development. The superintendent of the railroad, T. R. Gable, even went so far as to send out an exploring party that spent thirty days locating the minerals and a route to them for his train.[59]

The response to these reports was electrifying. John Wetherill, a trader to the Navajos, passed through Bluff noting that the quiet Mormon community had turned into a wide-open boom town after 10,000 gold-mad men had rushed into the country.[60] F. A. Hammond, a Mormon leader, claimed that from thirty to fifty people a day went through Bluff, bound for the gold fields.[61] One Bluff resident complained, "They [miners] did not stop at our farms and our orchards and our houses and lands, but located every foot of ground on the borders of the river. They did not take in the sand rock bluffs above the town but otherwise than that, they located every inch and foot—my house where I live, my little orchard, my lucerne patch, corn patch is all under placer claim."[62]

The Navajos reacted to these events by moving toward the river in large numbers and aggressively defending their lands. They drove the prospectors from the south side of the San Juan, destroyed claim markers, and scattered the miners' horses and burros.[63] Fortunately, when little actual wealth resulted, the gold rush died in 1893 and relieved the pressure on both Mormon and Navajo lands.

Interest shifted back to the Carrizos. In 1894, J. H. P. Voorhies and some mining associates requested authority to inspect some valuable veins of minerals in a volcanic tract of ground "of no possible use to Indians . . . and one which they will no doubt be very willing to cede to the government."[64] General A. McCook, writing to the Adjutant General of the Army, recommended approval, since he knew these men from the 1892 exploratory expedition. He further suggested they be allowed to take 1,000 pounds of ore for sampling. His positive response may have been influenced by the fact that Voorhies had connections with senators from Colorado and Indiana.[65] The government granted the lease in February 1896, but no action was taken to develop the mineral claims, presumably because Voorhies was called away to Colorado on business.

Interest continued to circulate around the Carrizos with reports that a party of 100 men was preparing to intrude onto the reservation in search of gold and silver. The agent dispatched two troops of cavalry as a preventive measure as much as to keep the Navajos pacified. While they were in the area, the soldiers also drove a group of Navajos out of the western end of the Southern Ute domain and back onto their own land.[66] The government approved another lease in 1901, this time for George F. Hull of Greensburg, Pennsylvania. He was given 640 acres with the understanding that if he found anything of value, (1) the Navajos would have a share of the profits; (2) they would be employed in the mine's operation; (3) and other prospectors would be kept out. Twenty Navajo headmen signed the agreement, and the company employed six Indians, each at five dollars a day, and also rented pack animals and teams. But the camp was too high, the threat of deep snows too great, the assays of ore unspectacular—so this venture, like all the others, was abandoned.[67]

At the same time as the San Juan gold rush and speculation on the Carrizos, yet another incident occurred in a series of unsettling events. On April 19, 1893, a Navajo man, Neesk'ahii (The Fat One), killed a trader named Welsh in Jewett. By April 24th, Agent E. H. Plummer took the offender into custody, but Neesk'ahii escaped, thanks to a poor performance by accompanying

Navajo police. Other Indians in the vicinity refused to help the authorities, were insolent, and were ready to stop the authorities if they made an arrest. Plummer sent for troops, causing the Indians' disposition to change. With a small group of Navajos, he was then able to put Neesk'ahii in the Aztec jail, but not before the threat of a lynch mob was quelled.[68]

Both sides involved in the incident had frayed nerves. The *Denver Republican* fostered discontent by printing information given by "a regular attache from Farmington" who claimed that "the whites have resolved to forever put a stop to the depredations of marauding red men," that the Navajos were preparing to "wipe out the little band of whites," that "Indian sentinels adorned every prominent hill on the south side of the river," and that Welsh was buried "in plain sight of hundreds of armed savages."[69] Large parties of men came from Farmington, Aztec, and Durango to provide assistance, reacting to accounts of trouble that had never occurred.

But not everyone was swept up in this movement. When Colorado's lieutenant governor, acting in the governor's absence, was asked what he was going to do about Navajo depredations in southwestern Colorado in general and the Jewett affair in particular, he replied, "I don't think there will be any need for us looking after those fellows. If the cowboys and the United States troops cannot take care of them, it will be time enough then to think of sending our troops down there. I've had enough of Indian fighting."[70]

The Navajos, however, were just as riled as the settlers. As soon as Plummer had his prisoner locked up, settlers notified him about more trouble in Jewett, this time at a besieged trading post owned by a man named Whyte. The problem started when a Navajo crossed to the north side of the river, left his pony with some friends, promised to return, but failed to do so. The friends heard some shots fired, assumed the Navajo had been killed, and decided that if the war had started, they were going to help it along. The missing man was later found, but not before tension increased.[71]

The settlers believed it was time to end the Indian problem on the north side of the river, so they sent word to Plummer that starting at noon on April 28th, there was going to be a roundup to drive the Indians back to the reservation. The agent was able to halt the movement by persuading the white men to leave this job to the cavalry. This incident reinforced Plummer's determination to try to have the Navajos' boundary shifted to the San Juan River, with no holdings to its north. He argued that there was no wood, water, or grass to draw them across, that the Indians became confused with survey lines and angles that were not tied to recognizable terrain features, and that a decrease of white-Indian contact on a daily basis would lessen friction. The Commissioner of Indian Affairs, D. M. Browning, disagreed with this analysis, stating, "If whites have found their way into that section of the reservation and are encroaching upon the Indians, they should be removed therefrom in order that the Indians may enjoy peaceable use and occupation of the land which rightfully belongs to them."[72] The matter was dropped.

Yet agency concern in developing the northern part of the reservation continued. As early as 1889 the Navajo Agency built a home for a resident farmer to live in the San Juan country and supervise ditch construction, crop development, and agent affairs in a region often cut off from the headquarters located 100 miles to the southwest.[73] Work progressed slowly during the first half of the 1890s but by 1900, when other parts of the reservation reported drought conditions so severe that crops did not even sprout, the ditches along the San Juan were "a great benefit to the people in that district."[74]

The years 1901 and 1902 saw increased survey activity for ditches, large and small, with the intent that 2,000 Navajos would eventually be located in permanent homes. One estimate even suggested that two thirds of the families on the reservation could have homes on the San Juan and become self-supporting.[75] Although these ideas completely ignored the social and economic realities of Navajo culture, they illustrate the hope that large field irrigation agriculture would act as both an economic and a civilizing boon to the Indian.

The other aspect of the process of bringing civilization to the northern Navajo frontier was education. In 1903, the government formulated plans to locate a school building eight miles below Farmington, near the main irrigation ditch that was expected eventually to water 3,500 acres.[76] The Navajo response was generally favorable. One Navajo leader, several years before the plans became a reality, said that if the agent built a facility so that the parents would not lose their children to distant boarding schools, they would have as many as 100 students enrolled, in direct competition with the agency school at Fort Defiance.[77]

Thus, by 1905 construction of an educational facility with a capacity of 100 students was under way, with an anticipated opening date of September 1, 1906. A subagency headquarters, under the direction of William T. Shelton, moved to the same location. It was given the responsibility of controlling a district of 5,000 square miles with an estimated population of 8,000 Navajos, on and off the reservation. This district included a small portion of land in the Montezuma Creek area of Utah, added by an executive order dated March 10, 1905.[78] Government and stability—in the form of agricultural endeavors, a school, and the new Shiprock Agency—were now a permanent feature of the San Juan country. Although there were still trials and conflict ahead, a semblance of order concerning boundaries, economic development, and education was introduced.

The changes that occurred with the Navajo on the northern part of the reservation between 1870 and 1905, appear to form three general phases, though exceptions can be found in each. In the first, from the 1870s to 1884, government officials recognized the value of the San Juan area. Because of turmoil in the northern parts of the reservation, however, decisive action remained more of a hope than a reality. Coupled with a high rate of turnover in agents, a huge geographical area to be supervised, and a multiplicity of problems, this left any development in the north tentative at best.

The second phase, ending in 1895, saw a climax, then a lessening, of these problems, since more attention had to be focused on the area. This was caused by well-established white settlements and mining interests, who wanted either protection for themselves or the authority to exploit natural resources. At the same time, the Navajos aggressively maintained control of their reservation lands and expanded beyond them in order to graze their herds and raise some crops. Conflict called forth judgment, resulting in the expansion of Navajo lands.

The final phase, 1895–1905, was a consolidation of Navajo gains through governmental means and a realization of at least part of the economic potential of the San Juan. With farming developments and the introduction of the Shiprock Agency, the Navajos' rights to the area were firmly established. Just as Nati'nesthani (He Who Teaches Himself) experienced trials in establishing his way of life on the San Juan, so too did the Navajos in the late nineteenth century.

8 / Conclusion

The northern Navajo frontier saw many changes during the period between 1860 and 1900. The type and quality of these changes depended on a variety of elements, including the different types of Euro-Americans the Indians had to face. Mormons, gentile settlers, cattlemen, traders, miners, and agents were all part of this collage. Yet the key to understanding the events of this era lies with the Navajos, who adapted their strategies to their opponents. Rather than passively accept white encroachment upon their lands, as did some Indians, the Navajos worked to obtain their desired ends.

An attitude of resistance, stopping short of war, was particularly important after the Navajos' defeat by Kit Carson in the 1860s. Those Navajos who remained at large in peripheral areas realized that friendship with the Paiutes, and eventually the Utes, was an important key to survival. The Utes had proved effective in ferreting out the Navajos, uprooting them from their homes and subsistence, and killing or enslaving those they captured. The Paiutes served as a protective link, not only in the immediate present by helping to hide Navajos, but for the future by establishing Navajo-Paiute and Ute-Paiute links of kinship.

Eventually, these bonds of relationship and trade connections developed into a restless peace among all three groups, so that by the 1880s many Euro-Americans believed they constituted a cohesive band of renegades. Trouble caused by this faction brought disclaimers from Ute and Navajo agents who either blamed those Indians not under their control or claimed these renegades were a small band of outlaws impossible to catch. The Native Americans added to the confusion by insisting upon their innocence while blaming one of the other groups when an incident occurred.

The Navajos were also confronted by two types of settlers—the Mormons and the gentiles. The former based their Indian policy on peaceful relations, especially when missionary fervor and religious zeal were at their peak. This is not to suggest that the Mormons were sensitive to Navajo needs, but that the Saints recognized their own vulnerability due to isolation and realized that cooperation was the wisest policy. Only a select handful of Mormons actually served as missionaries, learning the Navajo language, preaching the Mormon gospel, and baptizing converts. Some Navajo families accepted these beliefs, but as time and pressures brought changes in the Mormons' beliefs and practices, the Navajos increasingly lost interest. Subsequent friction ended in the expulsion of the Mormons from reservation lands.

With a less friendly and accommodating attitude, gentile settlers, such as Henry L. Mitchell, were interested in the Indians only when there was an opportunity to benefit from them. The Navajos' reaction to these settlers was an aggressive policy that ranged from grazing large herds of sheep over public lands to threats of armed resistance. The Navajos had learned their lesson from the 1860s and realized that a large-scale outbreak would bring the military upon them. Instead, they adopted intimidation and covert action as the most effective means to obtain their ends.

The Ute reaction was far different. Open warfare in the form of killing, mutilating, and stealing livestock paved the way for armed conflict. Although the Mormons avoided shooting incidents, the gentile settlers and cattle companies harbored little love for the Indians and, when confronted with theft, would either call in the cavalry or handle the affair on their own terms. This was one reason that in San Juan County, Utah, alone, the Indians killed some twenty settlers and cowboys between 1880 and 1900, but only one Mormon.[1]

Trading posts were a powerful force that drew the Navajos to the boundaries of their reservation. Whether involved in legal trade or the illegal purchase of arms, ammunition, and liquor, the Navajos flocked to the northern side of the San Juan River, much to the consternation of their agents. The stores thrived on the Indians' business, bartering for wool, blankets, silver, and hides in exchange for commodities. Both local and national economic trends affected the trading posts, but the most important factor for the Navajos is that these stores increased the Indians' dependence on Euro-American goods. Although the depression of the 1890s forced many of the posts to close, the Navajos continued to desire their products, so that as conditions improved in the early 1900s, a flourishing trade exploded on the reservation.

The final stage in the settling of the northern Navajo frontier came with the agents' official introduction of agriculture into this region. The Navajos had always recognized the San Juan River as a profitable and continuous source of water for crop raising, but some feared Ute and Paiute depredations, while others desired to be close to their agency, and still others had land too distant to make practical use of the river. But as Navajo population and livestock increased, the agents became seriously interested in developing the northern region into a more productive and settled area.

To do this, they first had to ensure that the lands occupied by the Navajos were clearly defined, protected from miners and settlers, and controlled by an agent. The first part of this challenge was accomplished by a series of executive orders that established Navajo title to the land and expelled Mormon and gentile settlers from homesteads along the San Juan and Little Colorado Rivers. The Indians helped in this process by aggressively defending their lands, using methods previously mentioned. Interest in mining increased in the 1890s and with it came tighter control by agents, cavalry, and Navajos, all of whom lent a hand in denying access to the reservation. Those miners who did venture on to Indian lands did so only by government and Navajo approval.

At this same time, the agents and private missionary groups launched efforts to establish large irrigation works to help the Indians feed themselves and to move them along the road toward civilization. Initial efforts proved frustrating but eventually bore results. By 1903, William T. Shelton created a subagency at Shiprock, New Mexico, to oversee agricultural efforts along the San Juan River, encourage the development of a boarding school, and enforce law and order in Navajo-white relations. This completed the process of firmly establishing under Navajo control the major landholdings in the northern part of the reservation.

To understand events in this frontier area, it is important to understand that the Navajos played an active role in determining their own destiny. While other Indian tribes were losing lands, the Navajos were gaining, to the point that they now have the largest reservation in the United States. Many of these land additions occurred in the late nineteenth and early twentieth centuries, and the majority of them were in the northern part of the reservation. The government, its agents, and other Euro-Americans helped procure official title to the land, but it was the Navajos who created the atmosphere and established the need that led to these additions. By pursuing an aggressive defensive policy, they generally avoided bloodshed, curtailed white encroachment, and expanded their own land base. The beginning of the twentieth century saw the Navajos firmly entrenched along the southern side of the San Juan River, determined to accept or reject elements of Euro-American culture as they deemed appropriate. In the years to come, the Navajos continued to prove that they were pawns to no one.

NOTES

Chapter 1

1. For examples of this general approach, see Ruth Benedict, *The Navajos* (Norman: University of Oklahoma Press, 1956); Clyde Kluckhohn and Dorothea Leighton, *The Navaho* (Cambridge: Harvard University Press, 1974); Peter Iverson, *The Navajo Nation* (Albuquerque: University of New Mexico Press, 1981); and Robert W. Young, *The Role of the Navajo in the Southwestern Drama* (Gallup: the Gallup Independent, 1968).

2. Iverson, p. ll; Garrick and Roberta Bailey, *A History of the Navajo: The Reservation Years* (Santa Fe: School of American Research, 1986), pp. 28, 104.

3. Klara B. Kelly, *Navajo Land Use* (New York: Harcourt, Brace, Jovanovich, 1986), p. 1.

Chapter 2

1. Washington Matthews, *The Mountain Chant: A Navaho Ceremony,* Fifth Annual Report of the Bureau of American Ethnology (Washington, D.C.: Government Printing Office, 1887), pp. 387–417.

2. See Katherine Spencer, *Mythology and Values: An Analysis of Navaho Chantway Myths* (Philadelphia: American Folklore Society, 1957), and Karl Luckert, *Navajo Mountain and Rainbow Bridge Religion* (Flagstaff: Northern Arizona University, 1977).

3. Matthews, p. 411.

4. Richard W. Stoffle and Michael J. Evans, "Resource Competition and

Population Change: A Kaibab Paiute Ethnohistorical Case," *Ethnohistory* 23 (Spring 1976): pp. 180–83.

5. See L. R. Bailey, *The Long Walk* (Pasadena: Westernlore Publications Press, 1982): Clifford E. Trafzer, *The Kit Carson Campaign* (Norman: University of Oklahoma Press, 1982): and Ruth M. Underhill, *The Navajos* (Norman: University of Oklahoma Press, 1956).

6. Isabel T. Kelly, *Southern Paiute Ethnography,* Anthropological Papers 69 (Salt Lake City: University of Utah Press, 1965), p. 60; Stephen C. Jett, "Testimony of the Sacredness of Rainbow Bridge to Puebloans, Navajos and Paiutes," *Plateau* 45 (Spring 1973): 54.

7. Kelly, p. 167.

8. Robert C. Euler, *Southern Paiute Ethnohistory,* Anthropological Papers 78 (Salt Lake City: University of Utah, 1966), pp. 32–56.

9. Catherine S. and Don D. Fowler, "Notes on the History of the Southern Paiute and Western Shoshonis," *Utah Historical Quarterly* 39 (Fall 1971): 103–5; Albert H. Schroeder, "A Brief History of the Southern Utes," *Southwestern Lore* 30 (March 1965): 59–63; William J. Snow, "Utah Indians and the Slave Trade," *Utah Historical Quarterly* 2 (July 1929): 67–73; and Euler, pp. 45–47.

10. Frank McNitt, ed., *Navaho Expedition: Journal of a Military Reconnaissance from Santa Fe, New Mexico to the Navaho Country Made in 1849 by Lieutenant James H. Simpson* (Norman: University of Olkahoma Press, 1964), pp. 192–93.

11. L. R. Bailey, ed., *The Navajo Reconnaissance* (Los Angeles: Westernlore Press, 1964), p. 89.

12. U.S., Congress, House, "Indian Hostilities in New Mexico," H. Ex. Doc. 69, 36th Cong., 1st Sess., 1860, p. 29.

13. U.S., Congress, House, "Mr. Rencher to Mr. Cass," H. Ex. Doc. 24, 36th Cong., 2d Sess., 1860, p. 17.

14. U.S., Congress, House, *Report of the Commissioner of Indian Affairs,* Colorado Superintendency, 1861, p. 102.

15. Sally Draper Bailey interview by Aubrey Williams, January 29, 1961, Doris Duke Collection #740, Special Collections, University of Utah Library, Salt Lake City, Utah (hereafter, papers from this file are cited as Duke #).

16. For fuller accounts of Hashkeneinii's life, see J. Lee Correll, "Navajo Frontiers in Utah and Troublous Times in Monument Valley," *Utah Historical Quarterly* 39 (Spring 1971): 145–61; Byron Cummings, *Indians I Have Known* (Tucson: Arizona Silhouettes, 1952), pp. 1–6; Charles Kelly, "Chief Hoskaninni," *Utah Historical Quarterly* 21 (July 1953): 219–26; and Charles Kelly, "Hoskaninni," *The Desert Magazine* (July 1941): 6–9.

17. For an explanation of the dynamics of wealth among the Navajo during a later period of history, see Robert S. McPherson, "Ricos and Pobres," *New Mexico Historical Review* 60 (October 1985): 415–34.

18. Kelly, "Hoskaninni," p. 9.

19. U.S., Congress, House, *Report of the Commissioner of Indian Affairs,* New Mexico Superintendency, 1864, p. 185.

20. U.S., Congress, *War of the Rebellion,* Series I, Vol. 48, Part I, Major E. W. Eaton to Captain Ben C. Cutler, February 8, 1865, p. 783.

21. *Ibid.*

22. U.S., Congress, *War of the Rebellion,* Series I, Vol. 48, Part I, General James Carleton to Headquarters Department of New Mexico, March 21, 1865, p. 1232.

23. *Ibid.*

24. U.S., Congress, House, *Report of the Secretary of the Interior,* "Report of Theodore H. Dodd—Navajo Agency, Fort Sumner, N.M., H. Ex. Doc. l, 39th Cong., 2d Sess., 1866, pp. 148–49.

25. David M. Brugge, "Vizcarra's Navajo Campaign of 1823," *Arizona and the West* 6 (Autumn 1964): 226–27.

26. See Walter Dyk, *Son of Old Man Hat* (Lincoln: University of Nebraska Press, 1938); Sally Clara Attakai interview by David M. Brugge, January 12, 1969, Duke #684; Hastiin Clau interview by J. Lee Correll, January 7, 1961, Duke #672; Frank Pierce interview by David M. Brugge, January 5, 1961, Duke #686; Curley Tso interview by Aubrey Williams, January 12, 1961, Duke #682.

27. Joe Attakai interview by Aubrey Williams, January 12, 1961, Duke #683; Billy Sawyer interview by J. Lee Correll, December 10, 1960, Duke #660; Mrs. Dan Tauchin interview by J. Lee Correll, December 10, 1960, Duke #659.

28. Charlie Begay interview by Aubrey Williams, Janurary 6, 1961, Duke #687; Paul Goodman interview by David M. Brugge, January 6, 1961, Duke #689; Dave Holiday interview by David M. Brugge, January 7, 1961, Duke #691; Tall Salt interview by Aubrey Williams, February 17, 1961, Duke #762.

29. U.S., Congress, House, *Report of the Secretary of War,* General Garland to Army Headquarters, H. Ex. Doc. 2, 35th Cong., 2d Sess., p. 282.

30. *Ibid.,* January 24, 1858, p. 281.

31. *Ibid.,* General Garland to General Johnston, March 13, 1858, p. 286.

32. U.S., Congress, Senate, *Report of the Secretary of War,* Colonel Bonneville to the General-in-Chief, S. Ex. Doc. 2, 36th Cong., 1st Sess., 1859, pp. 339–40.

33. Paul Jones interview by Aubrey Williams, January 19, 1961, Duke #712; George Martin, Sr., interview by David M. Brugge, March 22, 1961, Duke #913.

34. Maggie Holgate interview by Gary Shumway, June 13, 1968, Duke #956.

35. Erastus Snow to Captain R. N. Fenton, November 17, 1869, Record Group 75, Letters Received by Office of Indian Affairs, New Mexico Superintendency, 1870, National Archives, Washington, D.C. (hereafter cited as Letters Received—N.M.)

36. Captain F. T. Bennett to Major William Clinton, December 23, 1869, Letters Received—N.M.

37. Lieutenant Colonel D. S. Miles to Lieutenant John D. Wilkins, November 23, 1858, Record Group 98, Letters Received by the War Department, 1858, Navajo Tribal Archives, Window Rock, Arizona.

38. Major Albert Pfeiffer to A. K. Graves, December 10, 1866, Letters Received—N.M.

39. Felipe Delgado to Office of Indian Affairs, January 7, 1866; W. F. M. Arny to General Luther Webb, May 31, 1868, Letters Received—N.M.

40. Annual Report of the Abiquiu Indian Agency, *Report of the Secretary of the Interior,* August 31, 1868, pp. 626–29; W. F. M. Arny to Charles Mix, October 3, 1868, Letters Received—N.M.

41. W. F. M. Arny to Ely S. Parker, July 7, 1869, Letters Received—N.M.

42. J. B. Hansen to Major William Clinton, October 13, 1869; Captain F. T. Bennett to Major William Clinton, October 26, 1869, Letters Received—N.M.

43. Old Man Bob interview by Aubrey Williams, January 22, 1961, Duke #734; Eddie Nakai interview by Aubrey Williams, January 21, 1961, Duke #723; see also Broderick H. Johnson, ed., *Stories of the Long Walk Period,* (Tsaile: Navajo Community College Press, 1973), pp. 23–43, 210–13, 159–68.

44. Mabel Dry interview by Kay Fowler, July 18 and 25, 1967, Duke #106 and 110; Billy Holiday interview by Aubrey Williams, July 21, 1961, Duke #668; Billy Sawyer; Pat Shortfinger interview by David M. Brugge, January 11, 1961, Duke #694.

45. Kelly, "Chief Hoskininni," p. 225.

46. W. W. Hill, "Navaho Trading and Trading Ritual: A Study of Cultural Dynamics," *Southwestern Journal of Anthropology* 4 (Autumn 1948): 377, 380.

47. Dry, Duke #110, p. 23.

48. Shortfinger, p. 149.

49. Hill, p. 388.

50. William H. Jackson and Howard R. Driggs, *The Pioneer Photographer* (New York: World Book Company, 1929), pp. 238–40.

51. Dick's Sister interview by Aubrey Williams, February 23, 1961, Duke #912; Jim Mike interview by Aubrey Williams, January 29, 1961, Duke #916; Tall Salt; Frank Pierce; Maggie Holgate; John Daw; Joe Attakai; and Paul Goodman.

52. Census for 1928 through 1937, Consolidated Ute Agency, Ignacio, Colorado: Pahutes of Allen Canyon, Utah. Films #575, 769, Genealogical Section, Brigham Young University Library, Provo, Utah. See also "Supplemental Response on Behalf of the Navajo Nation to the Petition of Evelyn James Seeking Recognition of a 'San Juan Southern Paiute Tribe' " produced by Brown and Bain Professional Association of Phoenix, Arizona, September 9, 1985, for the litigation concerning Paiute/Navajo status of the San Juan Band. See pp. 19–28 and Exhibits G, I, R through X.

53. Annual Report of the Navajo Agency, *Report of the Commissioner of Indian Affairs,* 1872, p. 296.

54. Annual Report of the Los Pinos Agency, *Report of the Commissioner of Indian Affairs,* 1872, p. 290.

55. Annual Report of the Los Pinos Agency, *Report of the Commissioner of Indian Affairs,* 1873, p. 258.

56. Chandler Robins to Colonel L. Edwin Dudley, June 30, 1874, Letters Received—N.M.

57. Jacob Hamblin to W. F. M. Arny, March 7, 1874, "Correspondence

to Jacob Hamblin," Special Collections, Brigham Young University Library, Provo, Utah.

58. Pearson H. Corbett, *Jacob Hamblin: Peacemaker* (Salt Lake City: Deseret Book Company, 1952), pp. 343–57.

59. John R. Young to Brigham Young, May 20, 1874, "Mormon Settlements in Arizona," Special Collections, University of Utah Library, Salt Lake City, Utah.

60. Colonel Edward Hatch to Assistant Adjutant General, September 30, 1876, Letters Received—N.M.

61. *Ibid.*

62. Alex G. Irvine to Commissioner of Indian Affairs, March 7, 1878, Letters Received—N.M.

63. F. H. Weaver to Commissioner of Indian Affairs, April 22, 1878: "Correspondence: 1877–1939 Trespassers on Ute Lands," Consolidated Ute Agency Records, Federal Records Center, Denver, Colorado. S. Axtell to Carl Schurz, May 28, 1878, Letters Received—N.M.

64. Annual Report of the Los Pinos Agency, *Report of the Commissioner of Indian Affairs,* 1878, p. 16.

65. Galen Eastman to Commissioner of Indian Affairs, February 6, 1880, Letters Received—N.M.

66. H. L. Mitchell to Galen Eastman, February 15, 1880, Letters Received—N.M.

67. J. Carpenter to Carl Schurz, February 28, 1880, Letters Received—N.M.

68. H. L. Mitchell to Galen Eastman, February 27, 1880, Letters Received—N.M.

69. "Indian Imps," *Denver Tribune,* March 17, 1880, p. 4.

70. Captain F. T. Bennett to Acting Assistant Adjutant General of New Mexico, March 22, 1880, Letters Received—N.M.

Chapter 3

1. Christian L. Christensen, "An Indian Vision," 1881, Special Collections, Harold B. Lee Library, Brigham Young University, Provo, Utah.

2. For further information, see Albert R. Lyman, "The Fort on the Firing Line," *The Improvement Era,* October, 1948– March, 1950; Juanita Brooks, "Indian Relations on the Mormon Frontier," *Utah Historical Quarterly* 22 (January– April 1944): 1–48; Richard W. Stoffle and Michael J. Evans, "Resource Competition and Population Change: A Kaibab Paiute Ethnohistorical Case," *Ethnohistory 23* (Spring 1976): 173–97.

3. A number of books and articles have been written about Jacob Hamblin and his work among the Indians. Because of this, his role in southern Utah and northern Arizona will not be discussed to any great extent. For further information see Pearson H. Corbett, *Jacob Hamblin: The Peacemaker* (Salt Lake City: Deseret Book Company, 1973); Leland H. Creer, *The Activities of Jacob Hamblin in the Region of the Colorado,* Anthropological Papers Number 33, University of Utah, May 1958; Juanita Brooks, *Jacob Hamblin, Mormon Apostle to the Indians* (Salt Lake City: Westwater Press, 1980).

4. See Dan Vogel, *Indian Origins and the Book of Mormon* (Midvale, Utah: Signature Books, 1986).

5. See Charles S. Peterson, *Take Up Your Mission, Mormon Colonizing Along the Little Colorado River, 1870–1900* (Tucson: University of Arizona Press, 1973); James H. McClintock, *Mormon Settlement in Arizona* (Tucson: Universtiy of Arizona Press, 1921).

6. For further discussion of Navajo religion, see *The Handbook of North American Indians,* Volume 10 (Washington: Smithsonian Institute, 1983), pp. 502–91; Gladys A. Reichard, *Navajo Religion: A Study of Symbolism* (New York: Bollingen Foundation, 1950); and Evon Z. Vogt, *People of Rimrock: A Study of Values in Five Cultures* (New York: Atheneum, 1970).

7. Brigham Young to Elders Smith, Lake, Ballinger, and Allen, July 15, 1876, Correspondence to Lot Smith, Special Collections, Brigham Young University Library, Provo, Utah.

8. Elder Lorenzo H. Hatch to Editor of *Deseret News,* March 18, 1877, Papers of Lot Smith, 1855–89, Special Collections, Brigham Young University Library, Provo, Utah.

9. U.S., Congress, *War of the Rebellion,* Series I, Vol. 48, Part I, General James Carlton to Headquarters, Department of New Mexico, March 21, 1865, p. 1232.

10. Karl Luckert, *Navajo Mountain and Rainbow Bridge Religion* (Flagstaff: Museum of Northern Arizona, 1977), p. 103.

11. *Ibid.,* p. 5.

12. *Ibid.,* p. 48.

13. *Ibid.,* p. 70.

14. Bruce McConkie, *Mormon Doctrine* (Salt Lake City: Bookcraft Publishing Co., 1966), p. 21.

15. Leonard Arrington, *Great Basin Kingdom: An Economic History of the Latter-day Saints* (Lincoln: University of Nebraska Press, 1966), p. 7.

16. *Ibid.,* p. 39.

17. David E. Miller, *Hole-in-the-Rock* (Salt Lake City: University of Utah Press, 1966), p. 12.

18. Kumen Jones, "Writings of Kumen Jones," Special Collections, Brigham Young University Library, Provo, Utah, p. 140.

19. Miller, p. 12.

20. *Ibid.,* p. 3.

21. Kumen Jones, "The San Juan Mission to the Indians," Special Collections, Brigham Young University Library, Provo, Utah, p. 28.

22. Minutes of the Little Colorado Stake Quarterly Conference, January 27, 1878, Special Collections, Brigham Young University Library, Provo, Utah, pp. 14–15.

23. Brigham Young to Elder Lot Smith and the other Presidents of Companies, Little Colorado River, September 1876, Correspondence to Lot Smith, Special Collections, Brigham Young University Library, Provo, Utah.

24. The following works contain a number of entries emphasizing personal efforts to learn Indian languages: "Diary and Journal of James Stephen Brown"; "Diary of Christian L. Christensen"; and Albert R. Lyman's "History

of San Juan County, 1879–1917," all in Special Collections, Brigham Young University Library, Provo, Utah.

25. Christian L. Christensen, "Diary of Christian Lingo Christensen," Special Collections, Brigham Young University Library, Provo, Utah, pp. 9, 50–52.

26. Ammon M. Tenney, "Letters and Journal of Ammon M. Tenney," Special Collections, Brigham Young University Library, Provo, Utah, p. 18.

27. *Ibid.*, p. 21.

28. Christensen, p. 52.

29. *Ibid.*, p. 92.

30. *Ibid.*, pp. 92–93.

31. *Ibid.*, pp. 50–51.

32. W. Clinton to E. S. Parker, January 17, 1870, Record Group 75, Letters Received by the Office of Indian Affairs—New Mexico Superintendency, 1870, National Archives, Washington, D.C. (hereafter, correspondence from these files is cited as Letters Received—N.M.)

33. See books and articles previously cited concerning Jacob Hamblin, especially Corbett, pp. 343–57.

34. W. F. M. Arny to Colonel L. Edwin Dudley, February 16, 1874, Letters Received—N.M.

35. Jacob Hamblin to the Navajo Agent, March 7, 1874, Letters Received—N.M.

36. W. F. M. Arny to Jacob Hamblin, March 28, 1874, Letters Received—N.M.

37. W. F. M. Arny to Colonel L. Edwin Dudley, March 28, 1874, Letters Received—N.M.

38. Petition signed by twenty-one Mormons to Superintendent and Agent of the Navajo Agency, April 30, 1874, Letters Received—N.M.

39. Jacob Hamblin, Thales Haskell, *et al.*, to Chiefs of Navajo Nation, May 3, 1874, Letters Received—N.M.

40. W. F. M. Arny to Colonel L. Edwin Dudley, May 12, 1874, Letters Received—N.M.

41. W. F. M. Arny to Commissioner of Indian Affairs, January 14, 1875, Letters Received—N.M.

42. W. F. M. Arny to Colonel J. Irvine Gregg, June 3, 1874; Colonel L. Edwin Dudley to Edward P. Smith, June 19, 1874, Letters Received—N.M.

43. James S. Brown, "The Journal of James S. Brown" Special Collections, Brigham Young University Library, Provo, Utah, p. 1.

44. James S. Brown, *Life of a Pioneer: Autobiography of James S. Brown* (Salt Lake City: George Q. Cannon & Sons, Company, 1900), pp. 463–64.

45. Brown, "Journal," p. 19.

46. Brown, *Life,* p. 467.

47. Lot Smith to John Taylor, September 28, 1877, Papers of Lot Smith 1830–92, Special Collections, Brigham Young University Library, Provo, Utah (hereafter cited as Papers—Smith).

48. Lot Smith to Editor of *Deseret News,* April 28, 1876; Lot Smith to Brigham Young, August 28, 1876; Lorenzo Hatch to Editor of *Deseret News,* March 18, 1877, Papers—Smith.

49. Brigham Young to Brethren Smith, Ballinger, Lake and Allen, January 10, 1877, Papers—Smith.

50. Lot Smith to John Taylor, March 29, 1878; John Taylor to Lot Smith, April 17, 1878, Papers—Smith.

51. Christensen, p. 23.

52. Brigham Young and Daniel Wells to Elders Smith, Ballinger, Lake and Allen, July 15, 1876, Correspondence to Lot Smith, Special Collections, Brigham Young University Library, Provo, Utah.

53. Peterson, pp. 26, 106, 126.

54. Minutes of the Little Colorado Stake Conference, Special Collections, Brigham Young University Library, Provo, Utah, p. 177. Charles Peterson, in an endnote to these minutes, mentions that this is a remarkable harvest if the report is accurate but that no mention is made as to the role the Mormons played in achieving it.

55. Christensen, p. 39.

56. *Ibid.*, pp. 21–22.

57. U.S., Congress, *Report of the Secretary of War,* "Report of Major General John Pope," 48th Cong., 1st Sess. 1883, p. 134.

58. *Ibid.*

59. George A. McCarter to Robert T. Lincoln, June 7, 1884, Record Group 75, Letters Received, 1881–1907, Bureau of Indian Affairs, National Archives, Washington, D.C. (hereafter cited as Letters Received—BIA).

60. Thomas Perez to John H. Bowman, July 14, 1884; Bowman to Commissioner of Indian Affairs, July 18, 1884; Bowman to Commissioner, October 30, 1884, Letters Received—BIA.

61. Christensen, p. 74.

62. *Ibid.*, p. 162.

63. Lieutenant R. E. L. Michie to Assistant Adjutant General, Department of Arizona, July 13, 1892. Letters Received—BIA; David Brinkerhoff to J. N. Smith, June 23, 1892, Papers—Smith.

64. *Ibid.;* Thomas W. Brookbank to Honorable N. O. Murphy, August 2, 1892, Letters Received—BIA; D. M. Browning to Captain Constant Williams, July 13, 1895: Record Group 75, Bureau of Indian Affairs, Consolidated Ute Agency Records, Federal Records Center, Denver, Colorado.

65. For detailed reports of the conditions surrounding the Mormon-Navajo struggle for this area, see the following: U.S., Congress, House, "Agreement with Navajo Indians," H. Ex. Doc. 310, 54th Cong., 2d Sess., 1897, pp. 1–17; Major James McLaughlin to Secretary of the Interior, August 9, 1898, James McLaughlin Papers, Assumption Abbey Archives, Microfilm #23; U.S., Congress, Senate, "Enlargement of Navajo Indian Reservation in Arizona," S. Ex. Doc. 68, 56th Cong., 1st Sess., 1900, pp. 1–27.

66. Luckert, p. 118.

Chapter 4

1. See Ira S. Freeman, *A History of Montezuma County* (Boulder: Johnson Publishing Company, 1958).

2. H. L. Mitchell, E. B. Mitchell, John Bruer, and C. B. Jackson, "Evaluation of Property Destroyed in Kane County, Utah," December 24, 1879: Record Group 75, Bureau of Indian Affairs, Consolidated Ute Agency, Federal Records Center, Denver, Colorado (hereafter, correspondence from these files is cited as Consol. Ute Agency Records).

3. Mortality Records, Clerk's Office, Montezuma County Courthouse, Cortez, Colorado.

4. Freeman, p. 53.

5. Mitchell *et al.*, "Evaluation of Property Destroyed . . .," December 24, 1879, Consol. Ute Agency Records.

6. "San Juan Stake History," Special Collections, Brigham Young University Library, Provo, Utah, pp. 15–16.

7. "Life of Parley Butt," Special Collections, University of Utah Library, Salt Lake City, Utah, p. 4.

8. "San Juan Stake History," pp 20–21.

9. David E. Miller, *Hole-in-the-Rock* (Salt Lake City: University of Utah Press, 1959), p. 12; Kumen Jones, "Writings of Kumen Jones," Special Collections, Brigham Young University Library, Provo, Utah, p. 203.

10. Butt, p. 4; Miller, p. 156.

11. Albert R. Lyman, "History of San Juan County, 1879–1917," Special Collections, Brigham Young University Library, Provo, Utah, p.15.

12. "San Juan Stake History," pp. 46–47.

13. H. L. Mitchell to Ute Agent, December 4, 1879: Record Group 75, Letters Received by Office of Indian Affairs—New Mexico Superintendency, 1879, National Archives, Washington, D.C. (hereafter, correspondence from these files is cited as Letters Received—New Mexico).

14. H. L. Mitchell to Governor Thomas of Utah, December 27, 1879, Letters Received—New Mexico.

15. Affidavit of Henry L. Mitchell, December 24, 1879, Consol. Ute Agency Records.

16. Galen Eastman to Commissioner of Indian Affairs, February 6, 1880, Letters Received—New Mexico.

17. H. L. Mitchell to Galen Eastman, February 15, 1880, Letters Received—New Mexico.

18. J. Carpenter to Carl Schurz, February 28, 1880, Letters Received—New Mexico.

19. H. L. Mitchell to Galen Eastman, February 27, 1880, Letters Received—New Mexico.

20. Galen Eastman to Commissioner of Indian Affairs, March 8, 1880, Letters Received—New Mexico.

21. Captain F. T. Bennett to Acting Assistant Adjutant General of New Mexico, March 22, 1880, Letters Received—New Mexico.

22. H. L. Mitchell to Colonel Page, July 13, 1880. Consol. Ute Agency Records.

23. "Jessie M. Sherwood Writing about Mary M. Jones Life," Special Collections, University of Utah Library, Salt Lake City, Utah, p. 9; see also Lyman's "History" and Platte D. Lyman, "Diary of Platte D. Lyman," Special Collections, Brigham Young University Library, Provo, Utah.

24. Albert R. Lyman, "San Juan County History—Historical Sketches," Utah State Historical Society, Salt Lake City, Utah, p. 4.

25. Utah Works Progress Administration (WPA), "Historical Records Survey," Utah State Historical Society, Salt Lake City, Utah, p. 16; "Minutes of San Juan County Commissioners," Historical Sketches of San Juan County, Utah Historical Society, Salt Lake City, Utah, p. 6.

26. WPA, "Historical Records Survey," n. p.

27. "San Juan County Minutes," Minute Book 1880–1914, Utah Historical Society, Salt Lake City, Utah, pp. 26–29.

28. H. L. Mitchell to Secretary of Interior, January 15, 1883: Record Group 75, Letters Received by Office of Indian Affairs 1881–1907, Bureau of Indian Affairs, National Archives, Washington, D.C. (hereafter cited as Letters Received—BIA).

29. D. M. Riordan to Bureau of Indian Affairs, February 21, 1883, Letters Received—BIA.

30. Cass Hite to Galen Eastman, April 17, 1883, Letters Received—BIA.

31. D. M. Riordan to Commissioner of Indian Affairs, December 31, 1883, Letters Received—BIA.

32. Colonel Stanley to Warren Patten, August 31, September 1 and 2, 1883, Letters Received—BIA. Further investigation of this incident indicates that blame for the murder was later placed on a Navajo. See David M. Brugge's unpublished manuscript entitled "Navajo Use and Occupation of Lands North of the San Juan River in Present-day Utah," in author's possession.

33. For an account of this incident, see J. Lee Correll, "Navajo Frontiers in Utah and Troublous Times in Monument Valley," *Utah Historical Quarterly* 39 (Spring 1971): 151–61.

34. H. L. Mitchell and J. F. Daugherty to Fred L. Fickey, April 16, Letters Received—BIA.

35. Fred L. Fickey to John L. Thomas, May 26, 1884, Letters Received—BIA.

36. Fred L. Fickey to Commissioner Hiram Price, June 10, 1884, Letters Received—BIA.

37. Report of Herrero Segundo submitted to D. M Riordan, April 29, 1884, Letters Received—BIA.

38. Major R. H. Hall to Assistant Adjutant General at Fort Leavenworth, April 18, 1884, Letters Received—BIA.

39. Second Lieutenant J. F. Kreps to Major R. H. Hall, April 21, 1884, Letters Received—BIA.

40. Edgar O. Noland to D. M. Riordan, April 26, 1884, Letters Received—BIA.

41. Second Lieutenant J. F. Kreps to Major R. F. Hall, April 21, 1884, Letters Received—BIA.

42. Albert R. Lyman, "History," p. 38.

43. Platte D. Lyman, "Diary," p. 312.

44. Albert R. Lyman, *Indians and Outlaws* (Salt Lake City: Bookcraft, 1962), p. 62.

45. Second Lieutenant J. F. Kreps to Post Adjutant at Fort Lewis, May 1, 1884, Letters Received—BIA.

46. Captain H. H. Ketchum to Post Adjutant at Fort Lewis, May 20, 1884, Letters Received—BIA.

47. Captain Allan Smith to Post Adjutant at Fort Wingate, May 14, 1884, Letters Received—BIA.

48. Platte D. Lyman, "Diary," pp. 313–14; Albert R. Lyman, "History," pp. 39–40.

49. H. L. Mitchell to W. A. Clark, December 28, 1884, Consol. Ute Agency Records.

50. John Bowman to Commissioner of Indian Affairs, February 23, 1885, Letters Received—BIA.

51. John Bowman to Commissioner of Indian Affairs, September 10, 1885, Letters Received—BIA.

52. Petition from Citizens of McElmo County, December 16, 1886, Consol. Ute Agency Records; J. S. Carpenter and B. Gifford to C. F. Stollsteimer, May 17, 1887, Consol. Ute Agency Records; Petition of Citizens of McElmo County, January 30, 1888, Letters Received—BIA.

53. Jones, p. 203.

Chapter 5

1. For further information on land use, see W. W. Hill, *The Agricultural and Hunting Methods of the Navaho Indians,* Yale University Publications 18 (New Haven: Yale University Press, 1938); Anne M. Smith, *Ethnography of the Northern Ute,* Papers in Anthropology 17 (Albuquerque: Museum of New Mexico Press, 1974); Robert Euler, *Southern Paiute Ethnohistory,* Anthropological Papers 78 (Salt Lake City: University of Utah Press, 1966); and Ute Mountain Tribe, *Ute Mountain Utes: A History Text* (Salt Lake City: University of Utah Press, 1985).

2. See Peggy V. Beck and A. L. Walters, *The Sacred* (Tsaile: Navajo Community College Press, 1977); Richard Van Valkenburgh, *Dinebikeyah* (Window Rock: U.S. Department of the Interior, 1940); and Karl Luckert, *Navajo Mountain and Rainbow Bridge Religion* (Flagstaff: Museum of Northern Arizona, 1977).

3. For details concerning the size and operation of these groups, see Charles S. Peterson, "San Juan in Controversy: American Livestock Frontier vs. Mormon Cattle Pool," *Charles Redd Monographs in Western History* (Summer 1974): 45–68; Charles S. Peterson "San Juan: A Hundred Years of Cattle, Sheep and Dry Farms," *San Juan County, Utah,* edited by Allan Kent Powell (Salt Lake City: Utah State Historical Society, 1983), pp. 171–203; and Don D. Walker, "The Carlisles: Cattle Barons of the Upper Basin," *Utah Historical Quarterly* 32 (Summer 1964): 268–84.

4. David E. Miller, *Hole-in-the-Rock* (Salt Lake City: University of Utah Press, 1959), p. 55.

5. Peterson, "San Juan in Controversy," p. 63.

6. J. Lee Correll, "Navajo Frontiers in Utah and Troublous Times in Monument Valley," *Utah Historical Quarterly* 39 (Spring 1971): 145–61.

7. Albert R. Lyman, "History of San Juan County, 1879–1917," Special Collections, Brigham Young University Library, Provo, Utah, pp. 15, 33.

8. H. L. Mitchell, E. B. Mitchell, John Bruer, and C. B. Jackson, "Evaluation of Property Destroyed in Kane County, Utah," December 24, 1879: Record Group 75, Bureau of Indian Affairs, Consolidated Ute Agency Records, Federal Records Center, Denver, Colorado (hereafter, correspondence from these files is cited as Consol. Ute Agency Records).

9. Charles S. Peterson, *Look to the Mountains* (Provo: Brigham Young University Press, 1975), p. 57.

10. Cass Hite to Galen Eastman, April 17, 1883: Record Group 75, Letters Received by the Office of Indian Affairs 1881–1907, Bureau of Indian Affairs, National Archives, Washington, D.C. (hereafter correspondence from these files is cited as Letters Received—BIA).

11. Affadavit of twenty-three Bluff settlers to John H. Bowman, November 2, 1885, Letters Received—BIA.

12. Llewellyn Harris to Francis M. Lyman, May 16, 1880, Madeline R. McQuown Papers, Special Collections, University of Utah Library, Salt Lake City, Utah; also A. R. Lyman, "San Juan County," p. 15.

13. Albert R. Lyman, *Indians and Outlaws* (Salt Lake City: Bookcraft Press, 1962), p. 62.

14. A. R. Lyman, "San Juan County," p. 53.

15. Charles S. Peterson, *Take Up Your Mission* (Tucson: University of Arizona Press, 1973), pp. 22, 60.

16. A. R. Lyman, "San Juan County," p. 35.

17. Kumen Jones, "Writings of Kumen Jones," Special Collections, Brigham Young University Library, Provo, Utah, p. 167; also Cornelia Perkins, Marian Nielson, and Lenora Butt, *Saga of San Juan* (Salt Lake City: Mercury Publishing Co., 1968), p. 225.

18. Galen Eastman to Commissioner of Indian Affairs, September 27, 1881, Letters Received—BIA.

19. Lieutenant George M. Williams to Post Adjutant, Fort Lewis, December 11, 1889, Letters Received—BIA; T. J. Morgan to Charles A. Bartholomew, December 16, 1890, Consol. Ute Agency Records.

20. A. R. Lyman, "San Juan County," p. 35.

21. Platte D. Lyman, "Diary of Platte D. Lyman," Special Collections, Brigham Young University Library, Provo, Utah, p. 37.

22. A. R. Lyman, *Indians,* p. 42.

23. A. R. Lyman, "San Juan County," p. 21.

24. P. D. Lyman, "Diary," p. 279.

25. San Juan Cooperative Company Records, in possession of Gene Johnson of Blanding, Utah, p. 116.

26. Peterson, "San Juan in Controversy," p. 58.

27. For an excellent study of the ecological impact of herding livestock, see William Cronon, *Changes in the Land* (New York: Hill and Wang Press, 1983).

28. A. R. Lyman, "San Juan County," pp. 44–45.

29. Lyman P. Hunter interview by Michael Hurst, February 21, 1973, Special Collections, Brigham Young University Library, Provo, Utah, pp. 3–4.

30. Peterson, "San Juan in Controversy," p. 57.

31. Harold Carlisle to Charles F. Stollsteimer, June 12, 1887, Consol. Ute Agency Records.

32. For numerous examples of the cowboys' militancy, see A. R. Lyman, "San Juan County" and *Indians;* also Perkins *et al., Saga.*

33. The most complete coverage of the Pinhook Draw fight is in Faun McConkie Tanner's *The Far Country* (Salt Lake City: Olympus Publishing Co., 1976), pp. 115–46.

34. Don D. Walker, "Cowboys, Indians and Cavalry," *Utah Historical Quarterly* 34 (Summer 1966): 255–62.

35. Harold Carlisle to Charles F. Stollsteimer, July 13, 1887, Consol. Ute Agency Records.

36. John Hiorlls (?) to Charles Stollsteimer, August 5, 1887, Consol. Ute Agency Records.

37. John H. Bowman to Southern Ute Agent, July 24, 1885, Consol. Ute Agency Records.

38. John H. Bowman to Southern Ute Agent, August 1, 1885, Consol. Ute Agency Records.

39. W. M. Davidson To C. J. Bartholomew, January 17, 1890, Consol. Ute Agency Records.

40. Edmund S. Carlisle to W. M. Clark, October 1, 1884, Consol. Ute Agency Records.

41. E. T. Walker to Southern Ute Agent, October 24, 1882, Consol. Ute Agency Records.

42. John F. Tapping to William M. Clark, December 16, 1884, Consol. Ute Agency Records.

43. Edmund Carlisle to William M. Clark, December 30, 1884, Consol. Ute Agency Records.

44. U.S. Congress, House, *Report of the Commissioner of Indian Affairs,* Navajo Agency, 1884, p. 178.

45. D. M. Riordan to Commissioner of Indian Affairs, December 31, 1883, Letters Received—BIA.

46. Lieutenant Guy C. Howe to Captain E. M. Heyl, May 5, 1884; Captain E. M. Heyl to Asst. Adjutant General, Santa Fe, May 6, 1884: Record Group 75, Letters Received by the Office of the Adjutant General, 1881–89. National Archives, Washington, D.C.

47. F. W. Knoege (?) to Hon. Sec. Lamar, September 9, 1887, Consol. Ute Agency Records.

48. Henry L. Mitchell to William M. Clark, December 28, 1884; James F. Daugherty to Charles F. Stollsteimer, November 5, 1885, Consol. Ute Agency Records.

49. H. Price to Warren Patten, February 16, 1882; Patten to Price, February 28, 1883, Consol. Ute Agency Records.

50. C. E. Vandever to Commissioner of Indian Affairs, March 4 and September 19, 1890, Letters Received—BIA.

51. Frank Silvey, "Pioneer Personal History Questionnaire," Utah State Historical Society, Salt Lake City, Utah.

52. For a discussion of the issues surrounding Native American values and the fur trade see Calvin Martin, *Keepers of the Game* (Los Angeles: University of

California Press, 1978), and Shepherd Krech III, ed., *Indians, Animals and the Fur Trade* (Athens: University of Georgia Press, 1981).

53. Williams to Adjutant.

54. For examples of ritualisitic behavior, see Karl Luckert, *The Navajo Hunter Tradition* (Tucson: University of Arizona Press, 1975); also Hill, *The Agricultural and Hunting Methods of the Navaho Indians.*

55. Walter Dyk, *A Navaho Autobiography* (New York: Johnson Reprint Company, 1980), p. 40.

56. L. Richardson to Southern Ute Agent, September 1, 1886, Consol. Ute Agency Records.

57. Knoege to Lamar.

58. *Creede Candle* (Colorado newspaper), Volume 1, Number 32, page 1, August 12, 1892.

59. Citizens of Grand and San Juan Counties, Utah, to Governor A. L. Thomas, August 14, 1890, Letters Received—BIA.

60. Gordon Land to C. Bartholomew, October 13, 1892, Consol. Ute Agency Records.

61. W. Price to E. T. Walker, July 14, 1882, Consol. Ute Agency Records.

62. D. H. Watson to Jack Moss, November 4, 1935, Consol. Ute Agency Records.

63. Williams to Adjutant.

64. Frank Silvey, "History and Settlement of Northern San Juan County," Special Collections, Brigham Young University Library, Provo, Utah, p. 42.

65. Williams to Adjutant.

Chapter 6

1. The most complete coverage of the early trading posts is found in Frank McNitt, *The Indian Traders* (Norman: University of Oklahoma Press, 1962). While this book covers the growth of the prominent traders on the Navajo Reservation, little is said about the activity occurring on the periphery with unlicensed vendors. By the early 1900s, the "golden years of the trading posts" were ready to begin, both in terms of numbers and the amount and quality of influence that traders were able to exert upon the Navajo.

2. Testimony of John Francisco as sworn to before Mayor Edward Dalton of Parowan, Utah, February 22, 1870: Record Group 75, Letters Received by the Office of Indian Affairs—New Mexico Superintendency, 1870, National Archives, Washington, D.C.

3. U.S., Congress, House, *Report of the Commissioner of Indian Affairs,* Navajo Agency, October 1, 1876: Office of Indian Affairs, Department of the Interior, Washington, D.C., p. 110 (Hereafter cited as *RCIA*).

4. "Rules and Regulations Prepared in Conformity with the Preceding Provision of Law as Contained in Section 5 of the Act of August 15, 1876": Record Group 75, Bureau of Indian Affairs, Consolidated Ute Agency Records, Federal Records Center, Denver, Colorado, pp. 7–9 (hereafter cited as Consol. Ute Agency Records).

5. Frank Silvey, "Pioneer Personal History Questionnaire," September 10, 1936, Utah State Historical Society, Salt Lake City, Utah; Robert G. Athearn, *The Denver and Rio Grande Western Railroad* (Lincoln: University of Nebraska Press, 1962): 104–106.

6. D. M. Riordan to Commissioner of Indian Affairs, December 31, 1883: Record Group 75, Letters Received by the Office of Indian Affairs 1881–1907, National Archives, Washington, D.C. (hereafter cited as Letters Received—BIA).

7. These posts, moving from east to west along the San Juan, were owned by Owen E. Noland, Spencer, Henry L. Mitchell, Bluff Co-op, Amasa Barton, and William and Frank Hyde.

8. H. C. Adams to Indian Agent, Fort Defiance, April 22, 1893, Consol. Ute Agency Records.

9. W. W. Daugherty to Lieutenant Plummer, April 5, 1893, Consol. Ute Agency Records; Plummer to Commissioner of Indian Affairs, May 20, 1893, Letters Received—BIA; Plummer to Post Adjutant, June 29, 1893, Letters Received—BIA.

10. Lieutenant E. H. Plummer to Commissioner of Indian Affairs, May 22, 1893, Letters Received—BIA.

11. M. Armstrong to E. H. Plummer, June 2, 1893, Plummer to Commissioner of Indian Affairs, June 8, 1893, Letters Received—BIA.

12. H. C. Adams to Indian Agent, Fort Defiance, April 22, 1893, Consol. Ute Agency Records.

13. Williams to E. H. Plummer, November 18, 1893; W. A. Hunter to Plummer, December 11, 1893, Consol. Ute Agency Records.

14. Charles E. Vandever to Commissioner of Indian Affairs, September 6, 1889, Letters Received—BIA.

15. J. F. Daugherty to Ute Agent, June 7, 1886, Consol. Ute Agency Records.

16. Citizens of McElmo to Commissioner of Indian Affairs, January 30, 1888, Letters Received—BIA.

17. J. F. Daugherty to J. D. C. Atkins, September 19, 1888, Letters Received—BIA; W. W. Daugherty to Lieutenant E. H. Plummer, June 30, 1893, and July 7, 1893, Consol. Ute agency records.

18. H. C. Adams to Lieutenant E. H. Plummer, August 1, 1893, Consol. Ute Agency Records.

19. Constant Williams to Commissioner of Indian Affairs, January 26, 1895, Letters Received—BIA.

20. *RCIA,* Navajo Agency, September 1, 1877, p. 159.

21. *RCIA,* Navajo Agency, October 14, 1880, p. 132.

22. *Report of the Secretary of War,* "Report of Brigadier General Stanley," September 29, 1884, p. 122.

23. *Durango Herald,* October 25, 1890.

24. W. M. Davidson to Charles J. Bartholomew, January 17, 1890, Consol. Ute Agency Records.

25. *RCIA,* "Report of Farmer in Charge of Navaho Extension," August 28, 1905, p. 171.

26. William T. Shelton to Commissioner of Indian Affairs, December 5,

1913: Major James McLaughlin Papers, Assumption Abbey Archives, Microfilm #5, on file in the Denver Public Library, Denver, Colorado.

27. *Ibid.*

28. For a good explanation of Mexican and Southern Ute relations, see Frances L. Swadesh, *Los Primeros Pobladores* (London: University of Notre Dame Press, 1974). Pages 106–10 and 123–25 deal particularly with the liquor traffic.

29. *RCIA,* Navajo Agency, August 31, 1885, p. 155.

30. *RCIA,* "Sale of Liquor to Indians," 1894, p. 61.

31. *RCIA,* Southern Ute Agency, August 18, 1886, p. 50; *RCIA,* Southern Ute Agency, August 5, 1887, p. 16.

32. *RCIA,* Southern Ute Agency, August 22, 1901, p. 204.

33. F. W. Knoeges to Honorable Secretary Lamar, September 9, 1887, Letters Received—BIA.

34. M. Armstrong to C. F. Stollsteimer May 1, 1887; Jno. J. Davis to C. F. Stollsteimer, February 14, 1887; Porter Mitchell to U.S. Indian Agent, Ignacio, October 4, 1888; W. M. Davidson to C. J. Bartholomew, January 17, 1890, Consol. Ute Agency Records.

35. Office of Indian Affairs, Circular to Indian Agents, March 30, 1878, Consol. Ute Agency Records.

36. Office of Indian Affairs, Circular Number 67, May 10, 1881, Consol. Ute Agency Records.

37. D. M. Browning to Captain Constant Williams, September 19, 1895, and March 31, 1896, Consol. Ute Agency Records.

38. M. Armstrong to C. F. Stollsteimer, May 1, 1887, Consol. Ute Agency Records.

39. S. S. Patterson to Commissioner of Indian Affairs, June 20, 1888, Letters Received—BIA; *RCIA,* Navajo Agency, September 1, 1888, p. 152.

40. *Deseret News,* December 28, 1854. The claim that the Navajos were eating human flesh is highly unlikely given their fear of ghosts associated with the dead. Unlike some Native American tribes, they did not practice ritualistic cannibalism.

41. For further information on Jacob Hamblin and other Mormon traders, see Frank McNitt, *The Indian Traders;* Pearson H. Corbett, *Jacob Hamblin* (Salt Lake City: Deseret Book Company, 1973); Leland H. Creer, "The Activities of Jacob Hamblin in the Region of the Colorado," Anthropological Paper #33, Department of Anthropology, University of Utah, Salt Lake City, Utah; and Albert R. Lyman, "The Fort on the Firing Line," *The Improvement Era,* issued serially from October 1948 to March 1950.

42. *RCIA,* Navajo Agency, September 4, 1873, p. 133.

43. Oliver Huntington, "Personal Diary of Oliver Huntington," as quoted in Faun McConkie Tanner, *A History of Moab, Utah* (Moab: Times-Independent Press, 1937), p. 16; U.S. Congress, Senate, *Report of the Secretary of War,* Colonel Bonneville to General-in-Chief, S. Ex. Doc. 2, 36th Cong., 1st Sess., 1859, pp. 339–440.

44. Don Maguire, "The Third Arizona Expedition," Don Maguire Papers, Utah State Historical Society, Salt Lake City, Utah, pp. 145–46.

45. *Ibid.,* pp. 153–54, 157–62.

46. Thomas F. Hopkins to General O. B. Wilcox, December 17, 1887; S. J. Kirkwood to Commissioner of Indian Affairs, January 24, 1882, Letters Received—BIA.

47. Galen Eastman to Commissioner of Indian Affairs, February 8, 1882, Letters Received—BIA.

48. Christian Lingo Christensen, "Diary of Christian Lingo Christensen," Special Collections, Brigham Young University Library, Provo, Utah, pp. 72–73.

49. *Ibid.*, p. 76.

50. Kumen Jones, "Writings of Kumen Jones," Special Collections, Brigham Young University, Provo, Utah, p. 213.

51. Albert R. Lyman, "History of San Juan County, 1879–1917," Special Collections, Brigham Young University Library, Provo, Utah, p. 24.

52. Platte D. Lyman, "Diary of Platte D. Lyman," Special Collections, Brigham Young University Library, Provo, Utah, pp. 269, 276, 278.

53. *Ibid.*, p. 313; A. R. Lyman, p. 45.

54. Fred Fickey to John L. Thomas, May 26, 1884; Fickey to Hiram Price, June 10, 1884, Letters Received—BIA.

55. Jones, pp. 206–07, 219; Kumen Jones Manuscript, Special Collections, University of Utah Library, Salt Lake City, Utah.

56. Cornelia Perkins, Marian Nielson, and Lenora Jones, *Saga of San Juan* (Salt Lake City: Mercury Publishing Company, 1968), p. 68.

57. F. A. Hammond to Colonel P. T. Swaine, June 23, 1887: Record Group 90, Records of the War Department, Department of New Mexico, National Archives, Washington, D.C.

58. Jones, "Writings," p. 218; P. D. Lyman, "Diary," p. 294.

59. P. D. Lyman, "Diary," pp. 294, 301.

60. Jones, "Writings," p. 22.

61. A. R. Lyman, "History," p. 16; Jessie M. Sherwood, "Notes Regarding Charles E. Walton," p. 3, and "Writings About Mary M. Jones' Life in Bluff," p. 7, Utah State Historical Society, Salt Lake City, Utah.

62. Beatrice Nielson, "Early Bluff Days," Special Collections, University of Utah Library, Salt Lake City, Utah; A. R. Lyman, "History," p. 64.

63. John W. Redd interview by Gregg Maynard, July 27, 1973, Charles Redd Center, Brigham Young University Library, Provo, Utah; A. R. Lyman, "History," pp. 67–68.

64. Walter Dyk, *Son of Old Man Hat* (Lincoln: University of Nebraska Press, 1967), p. 56.

65. *RCIA*, "Destruction of Game by Indians," 1894, pp. 66–67.

66. *RCIA*, Ute Agency, July 29, 1874, p. 174.

67. Walter Dyk, *A Navaho Autobiography* (New York: Johnson Reprint Corporation, 1974), p. 40.

68. *Ibid.*, pp. 67, 69; G. W. Hayzlett to Commissioner of Indian Affairs, September 18, 1902, Letters Received—BIA.

69. *RCIA*, "Navajo Blankets," 1914, p. 36.

70. *RCIA*, "Indian Traders," 1903, p. 34.

71. Office of Indian Affairs, Circular Number 150, April 13, 1885.

72. *RCIA*, "The Indian Trader," 1905, pp. 27–30.

73. Dyk, *Navaho,* pp. 87, 95, 191.

74. *Ibid.*, pp. 102, 105; also for detailed accounts of John and Richard Wetherill's excavation of Indian ruins during which Navajo labor was used, see Frances Gillmor and Louisa Wade Wetherill, *Traders to the Navajos* (Albuquerque: Univeristy of New Mexico Press, 1953), and Frank McNitt, *Richard Wetherill: Anasazi* (Albuquerque: University of New Mexico Press, 1974).

75. For an explanation and documentation of this incident, see U.S., Congress, Senate, "Report on the Employment of United States Soldiers in Arresting By-a-lil-le and Other Navajo Indians," S. Doc. 517, 60th Cong., 1st Sess., May 25, 1908; U. S., Congress, Senate, "Testimony Regarding Trouble on Navajo Reservation," S. Doc. 757, 60th Cong., 2d Sess., March 3, 1909; U.S., Congress, Senate, "Decision Rendered by the Arizona Supreme Court . . . Indians Imprisoned Without Trial," S. Doc. 118, 61st Cong., 1st Sess., June 29, 1909; and J. Lee Correll, Bai-a-lil-le: *Medicine Man or Witch?* (Window Rock: Navajo Parks and Recreation, 1970).

76. Colonel George H. Hunter to Adjutant General, Department of Colorado, August 26, 1908: Record Group 393, U.S. Army Continental Commands 1821–1920, Department of Colorado 1905–1911, National Archives, Washington, D.C.

77. Captain E. A. Sturges to Adjutant, Fort Wingate, August 12, 1908, Letters Received—BIA.

78. Richard E. Klinck, *Land of Room Enough and Time Enough* (Salt Lake City: Peregrine Smith Books, 1984), p. 47; Charles J. Kappler, *Indian Affairs— Laws and Treaties* Volume III (Washington: Government Printing Office, 1913), pp. 407, 433, 491, 575.

79. U.S., Congress, Senate, "Survey of Conditions of the Indians in the United States: Hearing Before Subcommittee of Indian Affairs," 75th Cong., Part 34, August 19, 1936, "Navajo Trading," p. 18043.

Chapter 7

1. Washington Matthews, *Navaho Legends* (New York: Houghton, Mifflin and Company, 1897), pp. 160–94.

2. U.S. Congress, House, *Report of the Commissioner of Indian Affairs,* Navajo Agency, November 1, 1872: Office of Indian Affairs, Department of the Interior, Washington, D.C., p. 52 (hereafter cited as *RCIA).*

3. *RCIA,* Navajo Agency, October 10, 1872, p. 296.

4. *Ibid.*

5. *RCIA,* Navajo Agency, September 4, 1873, p. 271; *RCIA,* Navajo Agency, November 15, 1873, pp. 266–67; *RCIA,* Navajo Agency, October 1, 1876, p. 110.

6. *RCIA,* Navajo Agency, October 1, 1876, p. 110

7. *RCIA,* Navajo Agency, September 1, 1877, p. 159.

8. *RCIA,* Navajo Agency, August 3, 1878, p. 108.

9. *RCIA,* "Executive Orders Relating to Indian Reserves in New Mexico," 1886, pp. 350–51.

10. *RCIA,* Ute Agency, November 19, 1881, p. 335.

11. Captain J. B. Ivins to Post Adjutant, Fort Lewis, January 6, 1880: Record Group 75, Bureau of Indian Affairs, Consolidated Ute Agency Records, Federal Records Center, Denver, Colorado (hereafter, Correspondence from these files is cited as Consol. Ute Agency Records).

12. E. T. Walker to Frederick W. Pitkin, July 1, 1882, Consol. Ute Agency Records.

13. See J. Lee Correll, "Navajo Frontiers in Utah and Troublous Times in Monument Valley," *Utah Historical Quarterly* 39 (Spring 1971): 145–61.

14. Captain John Stowe to Colonel Henry F. Page, June 7, 1880, Consol. Ute Agency Records; T. C. Bryan to J. H. Bowman, July 17, 1885, Consol. Ute Agency Records; C. E. Vandever to General Carr, May 14, 1889: Record Group 75, Letters Received by the Office of Indian Affairs 1881–1907, National Archives, Washington D.C. (hereafter, correspondence from these files is cited as Letters Received—BIA).

15. H. Howard to Senator Teller, July 31, 1882, Letters Received—BIA.

16. *RCIA,* Navajo Agency, August 31, 1885, p. 155.

17. *RCIA,* Navajo Agency, August 14, 1883, p. 123.

18. *Report of the Secretary of War,* Department of the Missouri, October 2, 1883, p. 133.

19. J. D. C. Atkins to Secretary of the Interior, April 14, 1886, Letters Received—BIA.

20. For a detailed account of the political and military events of this incident, see Frank D. Reeve, "A Navaho Struggle for Land," *New Mexico Historical Review* 21 (January 1946): 1–21.

21. Report of General B. H. Grierson to Secretary of Interior, June 10, 1887, *RCIA,* p. 69.

22. S. S. Patterson to J. D. C. Atkins, February 25, 1887, Letters Received—BIA.

23. S. S. Patterson to J. D. C. Atkins, June 16, 1887, Letters Received— BIA.

24. J. D. C. Atkins to Secretary of Interior, November 3, 1887, Letters Received—BIA.

25. George W. Gordon to Commissioner of Indian Affairs, May 29, 1889, Letters Received—BIA; *RCIA,* "San Juan River Settlers—Navajo Reservation, New Mexico," p. 82.

26. Charles E. Vandever to Commissioner of Indian Affairs, September 6, 1889, Letters Received—BIA.

27. Charles A. Bartholomew to Charles E. Vandever, November 15, 1889, Letters Received—BIA.

28. Charles E. Vandever to Charles A. Bartholomew, November 22, 1889, Letters Received—BIA.

29. George W. Hayzlett to Commissioner of Indian Affairs, May 8, 1901; Commissioner to Hayzlett, August 4, 1901, Letters Received—BIA.

30. *RCIA,* Navajo Agency, September 3, 1884, p. 133.

31. *RCIA,* Navajo Agency, August 23, 1887, p. 174.

32. *RCIA,* "The Navajo Situation," 1892, p. 126.

33. U.S. Congress, Senate, "Conditions of the Navajo Indian Country," S. Ex. Doc. 68, 52d Cong. 2d Sess., 1893, p. 48.

34. Citizens of Farmington to Secretary of Interior, March 4, 1895, Letters Received—BIA.

35. Bluff Citizens to Secretary of Interior, September 5, 1902, Letters Received—BIA.

36. *RCIA,* "Irrigation," 1897, p. 30.

37. *RCIA,* "Report of the Board of Indian Commissioners—Address of Mr. Alfred Hardy," 1896, p. 1008.

38. *RCIA,* Navajo Agency, August 31, 1891, p. 310.

39. *RCIA,* "Report of Field Matron, Navajo Reservation," August 4, 1893, p. 113.

40. *RCIA,* Navajo Agency, August 17, 1894, p. 100.

41. *RCIA,* Navajo Agency, August 15, 1895, p. 120.

42. *RCIA,* Navajo Agency, August 4, 1893, p. 113.

43. *RCIA,* "Proceedings of the Board of Indian Commissioners at the 14th Mohonk Conference—Address of Mrs. Eldridge," October 14, 1896, p. 46.

44. *RCIA,* Navajo Agency, August 29, 1895, p. 118.

45. *RCIA,* "Proceedings of the Board of Indian Commissioners at the 13th Lake Mohonk Conference—Address of Mr. Alfred Hardy," October 9, 1895, p. 27.

46. See Charles Kelly, "Hoskaninni," *Desert Magazine* (July 1941): 6–9; and Charles Kelly, "Chief Hoskaninni" *Utah Historical Quarterly* 21 (July 1953): 219–26.

47. See Correll, "Navajo Frontiers," pp. 151–61.

48. Statement of William F. Williams to J. Lee Correll, May 22, 1929, in possession of author; also Billie Williams Yost, *Bread Upon the Sands* (Caldwell, Idaho: Caxton Printers, Ltd., 1958), pp. 125–37.

49. *Ibid.,* p. 134.

50. *RCIA,* Navajo Agency, August 9, 1889, p. 260; U.S. Congress, House, *Report of the Secretary of War,* "Report of Colonel Grierson," H. Ex. Doc. 1, Part 2, Vol. 1, September 1, 1889, pp. 179–81.

51. W. A. Smith to Governor E. S. Stover, October 21, 1890, Letters Received—BIA.

52. *RCIA,* Navajo Agency, August 22, 1890, p. 166.

53. *Albuquerque Citizen,* January 17, 1891.

54. *Durango Herald,* January 17, 1891.

55. *RCIA,* "Commissions and Negotiations for Reduction of Reservations," 1892, p. 75.

56. Walter Dyk, *A Navaho Autobiography* (New York: Johnson Reprint Company, 1947), p. 50.

57. U.S. Congress, House, "Navajo Indian Reservation," H. Ex. Doc. 201, 52d Cong. 2d Sess., January 25, 1893, p. 1.

58. *Ibid.,* p. 3.

59. *Ibid.,* p. 6; for a good overview of the events of this gold rush, see C. Gregory Crampton, *Standing Up Country* (Salt Lake City: Peregrine Smith Books, 1983).

60. Frances Gillmor and Louisa Wade Wetherill, *Traders to the Navaho* (Albuquerque: University of New Mexico Press, 1934), p. 43.

61. Cornelia A. Perkins, Marian G. Nielson, and Lenora B. Jones, *Saga of San Juan* (Salt Lake City: Mercury Publishing Company, 1968), p. 75.

62. *Official Report of the Proceedings and Debates of the Convention Assembled at Salt Lake on the Fourth Day of March 1895 to Adopt a Constitution for the State of Utah,* 2 Volumes (Salt Lake City: Star Printing Company, 1895), p. 1083.

63. *Salt Lake Tribune,* January 17, 1893.

64. T. M. Trippe to General A. McCook, September 22, 1894, Letters Received—BIA.

65. J. H. P. Voorhies to General A. McCook, September 21, 1894; McCook to Adjutant General of the Army, September 25, 1894, Letters Received—BIA.

66. Captain Constant Williams to Commissioner of Indian Affairs, March 26, 1896; Williams to Commissioner, April 24, 1896; David F. Day to Commissioner, May 9, 1896, Letters Received—BIA; also U.S. Congress, Senate, "Mineral Claims Navaho Indian Reservation, Arizona and New Mexico," S. Doc. 216, 56th Cong. 2d Sess., March 1, 1901, p. 3.

67. Lease by George F. Hull of Greensburg, Pennsylvania, July 17, 1901; also Jno. G. Worth to Colonel George F. Huff, November 15, 1901, Letters Received—BIA.

68. E. H. Plummer to Commissioner of Indian Affairs, April 27, 1893; Plummer to Commissioner, May 20, 1893, Letters Received—BIA.

69. *Denver Republican,* April 27, 1893.

70. *Ibid.,* April 26, 1893.

71. E. H. Plummer to Commissioner of Indian Affairs, May 20, 1893, Letters Received—BIA.

72. *Ibid.,* also D. M Browning to Plummer, May 3, 1893, Letters Received—BIA.

73. *RCIA,* Navajo Agency, August 9, 1889, p. 260.

74. *RCIA,* Navajo Agency, August 20, 1900, p. 192.

75. *RCIA,* "Navaho Reservation, Arizona and New Mexico," 1901, p. 65; Navajo Agency, August 16, 1902, p. 157; "Navaho Reservation, Arizona and New Mexico," 1902, p. 64; "Navaho Reservation," 1903, pp. 44–45.

76. *RCIA,* 7"Reports Concerning Indians in Arizona," 1903, p. 127.

77. *RCIA,* Navajo Agency, August 17, 1894, p. 99.

78. *RCIA,* "Report of Superintendent in Charge of Navaho on San Juan," August 12, 1905, pp. 267–68.

Chapter 8

1. Albert R. Lyman, *Indians and Outlaws* (Salt Lake City: Bookcraft, Inc., 1962), p. 42.

REFERENCES

Government Archives

United States. Congressional Records, 1858 to 1905. Brigham Young University Library, Provo, Utah.

United States. Official Records of the War of the Rebellion. Brigham Young University Library, Provo, Utah.

United States. Record Group 75. Consolidated Ute Agency Records, Bureau of Indian Affairs. Federal Records Center, Denver, Colorado.

United States. Record Group 75. Letters Received by Office of the Adjutant General, 1881–89. National Archives, Washington, D.C.

United States. Record Group 75. Letters Received by Office of Indian Affairs, 1881–1907, Bureau of Indian Affairs. National Archives, Washington, D.C.

United States. Record Group 75. Letters Received by Office of Indian Affairs, New Mexico Superintendency, 1858–1907. National Archives, Washington, D.C.

United States. Record Group 98. Letters Received by War Department, 1858. Navajo Tribal Archives, Window Rock.

United States. *Report of the Commissioner of Indian Affairs,* New Mexico Superintendency, 1858–1905.

Manuscripts, Papers, and Journals

Brown and Bain Professional Association. "Supplemental Response on Behalf of the Navajo Nation to the Petition of Evelyn James Seeking Recognition of a

San Juan Southern Paiute Tribe." Unpublished manuscript, dated September 9, 1985, in author's possession.

Brown, James S. "Diary and Journal of James Stephen Brown." Special Collections, Brigham Young University Library, Provo, Utah.

Brugge, David M. "Navajo Use and Occupation of the Area North of the San Juan River in Present-day Utah." Unpublished manuscript in author's possession.

Butt, Parley. "Life of Parley Butt." Special Collections, University of Utah Library, Salt Lake City, Utah.

Christensen, Christian L. "Diary of Christian Lingo Christensen." Special Collections, Brigham Young University Library, Provo, Utah.

Doris Duke Oral History Collection. Special Collections, University of Utah Library, Salt Lake City, Utah.

Hamblin, Jacob. "Correspondence to Jacob Hamblin." Special Collections, Brigham Young University Library, Provo, Utah.

Hunter, Lyman P. Lyman P. Hunter interview by Michael Hurst, February 21, 1973. Special Collections, Brigham Young University Library, Provo, Utah.

Jones, Kumen. Manuscript. Special Collections, University of Utah Library, Salt Lake City, Utah.

———. "The San Juan Mission to the Indians." Special Collections, Brigham Young University Library, Provo, Utah.

———. "Writings of Kumen Jones." Special Collections, Brigham Young University Library, Provo, Utah.

Lyman, Albert R. "History of San Juan County, 1879–1917." Special Collections, Brigham Young University Library, Provo, Utah.

———. "San Juan County History—Historical Sketches." Utah State Historical Society, Salt Lake City, Utah.

Lyman, Platte D. "Diary of Platte D. Lyman." Special Collections, Brigham Young University Library, Provo, Utah.

Maguire, Don. "Don Maguire Papers." Utah State Historical Society, Salt Lake City, Utah.

McLaughlin, James. "Major James McLaughlin Papers." Assumption Abbey Archives (microfilm), Denver Public Library, Denver, Colorado.

McQuown, Madeline R. "Madeline R. McQuown Papers." Special Collections, University of Utah Library, Salt Lake City.

Minute Book, 1880–1914. "San Juan County Minutes." Utah State Historical Society, Salt Lake City, Utah.

Minutes of the Little Colorado Stake Conference. Special Collections, Brigham Young University Library, Provo, Utah.

Minutes of the San Juan County Commissioners. "Historical Sketches of San Juan County." Utah State Historical Society, Salt Lake City, Utah.

Mortality Records. Clerk's Office, Montezuma County Courthouse, Cortez, Colorado.

Newspapers. *Albuquerque Citizen,* 17 January 1891. *Creede Candle* (Colorado), 12 August 1892. *Denver Republican,* 27 April 1893. *Denver Tribune,* 17 March 1880. *Deseret News,* 28 December 1854. *Durango Herald,* 25 October 1890; 17 January 1891. *Salt Lake Tribune,* 17 January 1893.

Nielson, Beatrice. "Early Bluff Days." Special Collections, University of Utah Library, Salt Lake City, Utah.

Redd, John W. John W. Redd interview by Gregg Maynard, July 27, 1973. Special Collections, Brigham Young University Library, Provo, Utah.

San Juan Stake History. Special Collections, Brigham Young University Library, Provo, Utah.

Sherwood, Jessie M. "Notes Regarding Charles E. Walton." Utah State Historical Society, Salt Lake City, Utah.

———."Jessie M. Sherwood Writing about Mary M. Jones—Historical Sketches." Utah State Historical Society, Salt Lake City, Utah.

Silvey, Frank. "History and Settlement of Northern San Juan County." Special Collections, Brigham Young University Library, Provo, Utah.

———. "Pioneer Personal History Questionnaire." Utah State Historical Society, Salt Lake City, Utah.

Smith, Lot. "Correspondence to Lot Smith." Special Collections, Brigham Young University Library, Provo, Utah.

———. "Papers of Lot Smith." Special Collections, Brigham Young University Library, Provo, Utah.

Tenney, Ammon M. "Letters and Journal of Ammon M. Tenney." Special Collections, Brigham Young University Library, Provo, Utah.

Utah Works Progress Administration (WPA). "Historical Records Survey." Utah State Historical Society, Salt Lake City, Utah.

Books and Periodicals

Arrington, Leonard J. *Great Basin Kingdom: An Economic History of the Latter-day Saints.* Lincoln: University of Nebraska Press, 1958.

Athearn, Robert G. *Denver and Rio Grande Railroad.* Lincoln: University of Nebraska Press, 1962.

Bailey, Garrick and Roberta. *A History of the Navajo: The Reservation Years.* Santa Fe: School of American Research, 1986.

Bailey, L. R. *The Indian Slave Trade in the Southwest.* Los Angeles: Westernlore Press, 1966.

———. *The Long Walk.* Los Angeles: Westernlore Press, 1964.

———. *The Navajo Reconnaissance.* Los Angeles: Westernlore Press, 1964.

Beck, Peggy, and Walters, A. L. *The Sacred.* Albuquerque: Adobe Press, 1976.

Benally, Clyde; Wiget, Andrew; Alley, John; and Blake, Gary. *Dineji Nakee' Naahane'.* Salt Lake City: University of Utah Printing Service, 1982.

Bingham, Sam and Janet. *Between Sacred Mountains.* Tucson: Sun Tracks and University of Arizona Press, 1982.

Brooks, Juanita. "Indian Relations on the Mormon Frontier." *Utah Historical Quarterly* 12 (January 1944): 1–48.

Brown, James S. *Life of a Pioneer: Autobiography of James S. Brown.* Salt Lake City: George Q. Cannon & Sons Company, 1900.

———. *Jacob Hamblin: Mormon Apostle to the Indians.* Salt Lake City: Westwater Press, 1980.

———, ed. *Journal of the Southern Indian Mission.* Logan: Utah State University Press, 1972.

Brugge, David M. "Vizcarra's Navajo Campaign of 1823." *Arizona and the West* 6 (Autumn 1964): 223–44.

Corbett, Pearson H. *Jacob Hamblin: Peacemaker.* Salt Lake City: Deseret Book Company, 1973.

Correll, J. Lee. *Bai-a-lil-le: Medicine Man or Witch?* Window Rock: Navajo Parks and Recreation, 1970.

———. "Navajo Frontiers in Utah and Troublous Times in Monument Valley." *Utah Historical Quarterly* 39 (Spring 1971): 145–61.

———. *Through White Men's Eyes,* Volumes III, IV, V, VI. Window Rock: Navajo Heritage Center, 1979.

Crampton, C. Gregory. "Military Reconnaissance in Southern Utah, 1866." *Utah Historical Quarterly* 32 (Spring 1969): 145–161.

———. *Standing Up Country.* Salt Lake City: Peregrine Smith, Inc., 1983.

——— and Miller, David E. "Journal of Two Campaigns by the Utah Territorial Militia Against the Navajo Indians, 1869." *Utah Historical Quarterly* 29 (April 1961): 149–76.

Creer, Leland H. "The Activities of Jacob Hamblin in the Region of the Colorado." *University of Utah Anthropological Papers* No. 33, 1958.

Cronon, William. *Changes in the Land.* New York: Hill and Wang Press, 1983.

Cummings, Byron. *Indians I Have Known.* Tucson: Arizona Silhouettes. 1952.

Downs, James. *The Navajo.* New York: Holt, Rinehart and Winston, Inc., 1972.

Dyk, Walter and Ruth. *Left Handed: A Navajo Autobiography.* New York: Columbia University Press, 1980.

Dyk, Walter. *A Navaho Autobiography.* New York: Viking Fund, Inc., 1947.

———. *Son of Old Man Hat.* Lincoln: University of Oklahoma Press, 1938.

Euler, Robert. "Southern Paiute Ethnohistory." *University of Utah Anthropological Papers* No. 78, 1966.

Faulk, Odie B. *Crimson Desert.* New York: Oxford University Press, 1974.

Fowler, Catherine S. and Don D. "Notes on the History of the Southern Paiute and Western Shoshonis." *Utah Historical Quarterly* 39 (Fall 1971): 95–128.

Freeman, Ira S. *A History of Montezuma County.* Boulder: Johnson Publishing Company, 1958.

Gillmor, Frances, and Wetherill, Louisa. *Traders to the Navajos.* Albuquerque: University of New Mexico Press, 1934.

Goodman, James M. *The Navajo Atlas.* Norman: University of Oklahoma Press, 1982.

Handbook of North American Indians—Southwest, Volume 10. Washington: Smithsonian Institute, 1983.

Hill, W. W. *The Agricultural and Hunting Methods of the Navaho Indians.* New Haven: Yale University Press, 1938.

———. "Navaho Trading and Trading Ritual: A Study of Cultural Dynamics." *Southwestern Journal of Anthropology* 4 (Autumn 1948): 371–96.

Hoffman, Virginia. *Navajo Biographies,* Volume I. Phoenix: Navajo Curriculum Press, 1974.

Iverson, Peter. *The Navajo Nation.* Albuquerque: University of New Mexico Press, 1981.

Jackson, William H., and Driggs, Howard W. *The Pioneer Photographer.* New York: World Book Company, 1929.

Jett, Stephen. "Testimony of the Sacredness of Rainbow Bridge to Puebloans, Navajos and Paiutes." *Plateau* 45 (Spring 1973): 133–42.

Johnson, Broderick H., ed. *Stories of the Long Walk Period.* Tsaile: Navajo Community College Press, 1973.

———. *Stories of Traditional Navajo Life and Culture.* Tsaile: Navajo Community College Press, 1977.

Judd, B. Ira. "Tuba City, Mormon Settlement." *The Journal of Arizona History* 10 (Spring 1969): 37–42.

Kappler, Charles J. *Indian Affairs—Laws and Treaties,* Volume III. Washington: Government Printing Office, 1913.

Kelly, Charles. "Chief Hoskaninni." *Utah Historical Quarterly* 21 (July 1953): 219–26.

———. "Hoskaninni." *The Desert Magazine* (July 1941): 6–9.

Kelly, Isabel T. "Southern Paiute Ethnography." *University of Utah Anthropological Papers* No. 69, 1965.

Kelly, Klara B. *Navajo Land Use.* New York: Harcourt, Brace, Jovanovich, Publishers, 1986.

Kelly, Lawrence. *Navajo Roundup: Selected Correspondence of Kit Carson's Expedition Against the Navajo, 1863–1865.* Boulder: Pruett Publishing Company, 1970.

Klinck, Richard E. *Land of Room Enough and Time Enough.* Salt Lake City: Peregrine Smith, Inc., 1984.

Kluckhohn, Clyde, and Leighton, Dorothea. *The Navaho.* Cambridge: Harvard University Press, 1974.

Krech, Shepherd, III. *Indians, Animals and the Fur Trade.* Athens: University of Georgia Press, 1981.

Luckert, Karl. *The Navajo Hunter Tradition.* Tucson: University of Arizona Press, 1975.

———. *Navajo Mountain and Rainbow Bridge Religion.* Flagstaff: Museum of Northern Arizona, 1977.

Lyman, Albert R. "The Fort on the Firing Line." *The Improvement Era* serially, October 1948 to March 1950.

———. *Indians and Outlaws.* Salt Lake City: Bookcraft, Inc., 1962.

Manners, Robert A. *Southern Paiute and Chemehuevi: An Ethnohistorical Report.* New York: Garland Publishing, Inc., 1974.

Martin, Calvin. *Keepers of the Game.* Los Angeles: University of California Press, 1978.

Matthews, Washington. "The Mountain Chant—A Navaho Ceremony." *Fifth Annual Report of the Bureau of Ethnology,* 1887.

———. *Navaho Legends.* New York: Houghton, Mifflin and Company, 1897.

McClintock, James H. *Mormon Settlement in Arizona.* Tucson: University of Arizona Press, 1921.

McConkie, Bruce R. *Mormon Doctrine.* Salt Lake City: Bookcraft Publishing Company, 1966.

McNitt, Frank. *Indian Traders.* Norman: University of Oklahoma Press, 1962.

———. *Navajo Expedition: Journal of a Military Reconnaissance from Santa Fe,*

New Mexico to the Navajo Country Made in 1849 by Lieutenant James H. Simpson. Norman: University of Oklahoma Press, 1964.

———. *Richard Wetherill: Anasazi.* Albuquerque: University of New Mexico Press, 1966.

———. *Navajo Wars, Military Campaigns, Slave Raids and Reprisals.* Albuquerque: University of New Mexico Press, 1972.

McPherson, Robert S. "Ricos and Pobres." *New Mexico Historical Review* 60 (October 1985): 415–34.

Miller, David E. *Hole-in-the-Rock.* Salt Lake City: University of Utah Press, 1959.

Olsen, Robert W., Jr. "Pipe Spring, Arizona, and Thereabouts." *The Journal of Arizona History* 6 (Spring 1965): 11–20.

Ortiz, Alfonso, ed. *Handbook of North American Indians,* Volume 10. Washington: Smithsonian Institution, 1983.

Perkins, Cornelia; Nielson, Marian G.; and Jones, Lenora B. *The Saga of San Juan.* Salt Lake City: Mercury Publishing Company, 1957.

Peterson, Charles S. *Look to the Mountains.* Provo: Brigham Young University Press, 1975.

———. "San Juan in Controversy: American Livestock Frontier vs. Mormon Cattle Pool." *Charles Redd Monographs in Western History* (Summer 1974): 45–68.

———. *Take Up Your Mission: Mormon Colonizing Along the Little Colorado River, 1870–1900.* Tucson: University of Arizona Press, 1973.

Poll, Richard D., Alexander, Thomas G.; Campbell, Eugene E., and Miller, David E. *Utah's History.* Provo: Brigham Young University Press, 1978.

Powell, Allan Kent, ed. *San Juan County.* Salt Lake City: Utah State Historical Society, 1983.

Reeve, Frank D. "The Federal Indian Policy in New Mexico, 1858–1880." *New Mexico Historical Review* 11–13 (July 1937 to July 1938).

———. "A Navaho Struggle for Land." *New Mexico Historical Review* 21 (January 1946): 1–21.

Reichard, Gladys A. *Navaho Religion: A Study of Symbolism.* New York: Bollingen Foundation, 1950.

Rusho, W. L., and Crampton, C. Gregory. *Desert River Crossing.* Salt Lake City" Peregrine Smith, Inc., 1981.

Schroeder, Albert H. "A Brief History of the Southern Utes." *Southwestern Lore* 30 (March 1965): 53–78.

Shepardson, Mary, and Hammond, Blodwen. *The Navajo Mountain Community.* Berkeley: University of California Press, 1970.

Smith, Anne M. "Ethnography of the Northern Ute." *University of New Mexico Anthropological Papers* No. 17, 1974.

Snow, William J. "Utah Indians and the Slave Trade." *Utah Historical Quarterly* 2 (July 1929): 66–90.

Spencer, Katherine. *Mythology and Values: An Analysis of Navaho Chantway Myths.* Philadelphia: American Folklore Society, 1957.

Stoffle, Richard W., and Evans, Michael J. "Resource Competition and Population Change: A Kaibab Paiute Ethnohistorical Case." *Ethnohistory* 23 (Spring 1976): 173–97.

Swadesh, Frances L. *Los Primeros Pobladores.* London: University of Notre Dame Press, 1974.

Tanner, Faun McConkie. *The Far Country: A Regional History of Moab and La Sal, Utah.* Salt Lake City: Olympus Publishing Company, 1976.

———. *A History of Moab Utah.* Moab: Times-Independent Press, 1937.

Thompson, Gerald H. *The Army and the Navajo.* Tucson: University of Arizona Press, 1976.

Trafzer, Clifford E. *The Kit Carson Campaign.* Norman: University of Oklahoma Press, 1982.

Underhill, Ruth. *The Navajos.* Norman University of Oklahoma Press, 1956.

Ute Mountain Ute Tribe. *Ute Mountain Utes: A History Text.* Salt Lake City: University of Utah Press, 1985.

Van Valkenburgh, Richard. *Dinebikeyah.* Window Rock: United States Department of the Interior, 1940.

Vogel, Dan. *Indian Origins and the Book of Mormon.* Midvale, Utah: Signature Books, 1986.

Vogt, Evon Z. *People of Rimrock: A Study of Values in Five Cultures.* New York: Atheneum, 1970.

Wagner, Marilyn R. "Navajo Settlement Patterns, 1846–1870: A Geographical History." M.A. thesis, University of Utah, 1978.

Walker, Don D. "The Carlisles: Cattle Barons of the Upper Basin." *Utah Historical Quarterly* 32 (Summer 1964): 268–84.

———. "Cowboys, Indians and Cavalry." *Utah Historical Quarterly* 34 (Summer 1966): 255–62.

Yost, Billie Williams. *Bread Upon the Sands.* Caldwell: Caxton Printers, Ltd., 1958.

Young, Robert W. *The Role of the Navajo in the Southwestern Drama.* Gallup: Gallup Independent and Robert W. Young, 1968.

——— and Morgan William. *Navajo Historical Selections.* Lawrence: Bureau of Indian Affairs, 1954.

Index